Sara J. McConnell

Selections of Poems and Prose

Sara J. McConnell

Selections of Poems and Prose

ISBN/EAN: 9783337369958

Printed in Europe, USA, Canada, Australia, Japan

Cover: Foto ©Thomas Meinert / pixelio.de

More available books at **www.hansebooks.com**

SELECTIONS

OF

Poems and Prose.

BY

SARA J. McCONNELL,
Allegheny City, Pa.

PITTSBURGH, PA.
PERCY F. SMITH PRINTING AND LITHOGRAPHING COMPANY, 204-206 WOOD STREET.
1893.

SELECTIONS OF POEMS

——BY——

SARA J. McCONNELL,

ALLEGHENY, PA.

THE MILLER OF NEWBERRY BRAES.

A New Version of an Old Song.

"There was an old miller in Newberry Braes,
Had a wicked old wife made him tired of his days."
In the length of the land, in the breadth of the town,
Whichever way she went up or went down,
It rattled like thunder, it clattered like hail,
The heart-broken people looked haggard and pale,
And the wretched old miller's poor wits went adrift
In this raging tornado sans let up or lift.

His teeth down his throat, his hair jerked from his head,
He dare sit on no chair or lie down in a bed.
Too weary to groan, too weak to shed tears.
Or wink with his eyes—he hadn't shut them for years,
At long and at last he no more could endure.
Said he, "Where she came from I'll take her back sure."
"So he shouldered his wife like a peddler his pack,
And, true to his word, he toted her back."

When they got there 'twas late in the fall,
A strapping big demon looked over the wall,
And seeing two creatures looked awfully queer,
Cried, "Get you gone both, we've enough like you here."
Then this savage old woman, she planted such blows
On the top of his head and the end of his nose,
That the smear of his brains ran out at his toes
Down over the wall and ruined her clothes.

A legion of demons rushed out to the fray;
This made the old woman more lively and gay.
Imp, demon and fiend, row upon row,
Like sheaves in a field she soon laid them low,
Till Beelzebub's self loud as he could bray
Ran howling to Satan, "Oh, send her away.
If you don't stop this woman, she'll clean out the place
And wipe up the floor with the last of our race."
So Satan was fain to the miller to call,
"Please don't, Mr. Miller, let your wife kill us all."

Hope turned to despair. He shouldered his pack,
And raving and swearing set out to go back;
Crying, "Fly for your lives, for I'm blessed with a curse.
My wife's been to hell and she's forty times worse."
Oh! Lord, cried the people who lived about there,
What will become of us? She's back, I declare!

When she called for the tea she had left in her pot,
The wretched inhabitants cursing their lot,
To present or future giving no thought,
In the wildest disorder got up and got.
They took to the woods, they fled to the hills,
They hid in the mountains, and said, "If God wills
We perish of hunger, right willing are we,
To what we have suffered it nothing can be."

Nor ever again in all their born days,
Did they ever return to Newberry Braes;
Nor ever a creature dare live in that town
Until that old woman lay dead in the ground.

DEATH'S ECLIPSE.

Oh, thou wilt come no more,
Never, never, never, never.
—*Shakespeare.*

Oh, thou wilt never, never wake.
No lapse of time the silence break
That seals thy lips.

No summer sunbeam ever warm
To pliant life thy rigid form,
Prostrate in death's eclipse.

And I, to-morrow, must I press
My lips to thine, in my long, last
Farewell to thee?

From the still churchyard all alone
Must I come back, and set me down
In this blank desolation Home?
It never more can be.

My daughter, Oh: my daughter fair,
Lit with the sunshine of thy hair,
'Twas paradise, Alas!

Joy's ecstasy and hope's despair,
And earth and heaven divided were,
By its gold radiance; daughter, where
It shines to-day, thou hast

Measureless, immortal gain,
Through my infinite loss and pain
Of breaking heart and aching brain.
Oh, ever more to me.

Blank, rayless, black as a cheron,
Our once so dear, so happy home,
And the pathway I must tread alone
To Heaven and to thee.

A CONTROVERSY.

Lady—Fleeting shadow of the springtime that left us
        yesterday,
      Evanescent gleam of roses, Oh! Summer, tarry,
        stay;
      Stay and close your opening lilies, 'twill detain
        you but a day.

Summer—If for the lillies and for you I was too short,
        woman, dear,
      Autumn will be all too long and to-morrow
        'twill be here.

Lady—What, autumn on to-morrow! Oh, how the
        years fly.
      The years that never reconcile Cameron and I.

Summer—"Procrastination," Lady, "is the thief of
        time."
      They who tarry for the future lose the present
        golden wine.
      Was it "hope deferred" estranged him. Why
        no answer, Lady, mine?

Lady—Keep the thorns to scourge the happy who culled
  your roses fair;
  I was all too wretched, Summer, to gather them
  or wear
  Their beauty on my bosom or their fragrance in
  my hair.

Summer—I brought my lovely roses for all the world,
  Lady,
  If you could or would not wear them, why
  chide you thus with me?

Lady—In the dreariness of winter I doubted not the
  spring,
  With its violets and zephyrs, would my truant
  lover bring;
  But most of all I trusted to your long, bright,
  sunny day,
  To chase with golden sunshine the last dark
  cloud away.

Summer—Ah, well, confiding Lady, at least it did for
  him,
  His happy honey moon not a cloud does dim,

Lady—His honey moon, Oh, Summer, if to-morrow
  autumn be,
  It could just as well be winter, 'twould be all
  the same to me—
  To the inmate of a madhouse what can change
  of season be?

And the summer went to-morrow and to-morrow
  autumn came,
And lit the sombre greenwood with a sheet of scarlet
  flame.
And the winter came, how icy and it brought an icy
  bier
To a madhouse where a woman lay dying with the
  year.
And the new year came and buried in the snow the old
  year's dead.
To the scanty crowd and wearied, "Dust to dust," the
  preacher said—
Standing in the snow he said it o'er the frozen earth
  they tossed
Down upon the shrouded nothing who all consciousness
  had lost
Of her present, past or future, of all travail 'neath the
  sun,
Cared for nothing under heaven, no, not even for
  Cameron.

THE INEVITABLE.

Jenny, poor girl, in a faded gown,
One summer morning went to town,
"This old dress," said she, "is a perfect show,
And this bonnet a perfect fright I know.

"What shall I do if I happen to meet
Any one that I know upon the street?"
And she thinks her life all bitterness;
And her fair young face looks dire distress.

On another branch of the self-same road
Johnny set out with a heavy load,
And a poor old horse, the very same day,
For the very same town, I need hardly say.

"This," said he, "is the darndest road
To drive an old horse with a heavy load;
I wish I was in Dixie myself, and he
On the other side o' Jordan, for all me."

Quarrelling both as they went, with fate;
Fretting both, at their low estate;
They turn a corner and meet, ah, me!
He is sore ashamed and so is she

But the poor old horse and his heavy load—
Had a long, long rest in the dusty road.
For an old oak tree is a splendid shade
And velvet never a carpet made

Softer than the grass that grew
Under that oak tree where the two—
Such is life—grew exceeding fair
In each others eyes, as they sat there.

Bonnet or gown? Their rustic trim
Grew nothing at all to her or him.
They only planned how from that day
They should hand in hand tread life's highway.

Contented under a double load,
They now tramp down a far dustier road;
Crying children run before,
Others follow crabbed, foot sore.

Homely clothing and homely fare,
Hard, dirty work, for them everywhere;
But their poverty is blessed with the wealth
Of earth's greatest riches—hardy health.

And if their burdens sore oppress,
Those burdens make their happiness.
If not, I must and do declare
Nobody has any anywhere.

PSYCHOLOGIC MUSINGS.

So I, after all, am nothing
  But a flash of consciousness,
On aggregated atoms
  Holden in chance duress

By the subtle influences
  That pervade infinite space
That the veriest of atoms
  And the vastest worlds embrace.

Omniscient, omnipresent forces,
  That with infinite alchemy
Build up the rocks of ages
  And wear continents away,

Upheave the mountain ranges
  With the earthquake's quivering shock.
Earth itself, those forces
  Can like a cradle rock.

They rule all suns, all systems,
  Each ponderous orb of light,
Impel resistless onward,
  In everlasting flight.

Yet are the violet's perfume,
  And the beauty of the rose,
The amber dawn of morning,
  And the evenings gorgeous close.

They bring to-day's brief hours
  That to-morrow come again,
To drop into the ages,
  As silently as rain.

Equipoised those subtle forces
  Make my life and me,
Their equilibrium broken
  I shall cease to be.

Oh, Heaven, Heaven, Heaven,
  Oh, ruined, "bankrupt faith,"
The total sum of living
  Is the nothingness of death.

Oh, vainest of delusions,
  What avails it me?
I thought my life's lost treasures
  Safe garnered up in thee.

Blank, blank annihilation,
  For them; Ah, then, for me,
I ask no other guerdon,
  Or other destiny.

As the dauntless hero marches
  Into the fiery breath
Of the cannon that belches
  Inevitable death,

Into the Cimmerian darkness
Brooding over all,
I march without a shudder.
Why should it appall?

'Tis the lot of all the living,
Undoubtedly 'tis best,
And the safety of oblivion
Is everlasting rest.

BIRDS OF PASSAGE.

[To the memory of a beloved only brother.]

Hear you the birds of passage crying?
Through the night and darkness they are flying,
Southward through the mist that hars
The sleeping world from the shining stars.

And they will alight at dawn of day
By some still lagoon or lonely bay;
Or their weary wings in some leafy brake
That casts shadows green o'er a quiet lake,
Fold to rest after their long flight
From the arctic winter's frigid night.

Spring after spring they have northward sped,
Autumn on autumn southward fled.
Screaming come and screaming go
'Twixt the tropic flowers and the arctic snow.

Over our heads they fly, but we,
Who oftimes hear, but seldom see
The fugitives whose midnight path,
Is a long highway 'twixt life and death.

'Twixt life and death, and with a sigh,
We watch our birds of passage fly,
With trembling haste in the wild birds' wake,
To the orange bower by the quiet lake.

From winter's snow and winter's rain
They fly in dread. They will come again,
They always say, when the violets come;
With the birds of passage they will hasten home.

Alack! for we know that no coming spring,
The poor fugitives will ever bring,
Whose weary wings 'mid tropic flowers,
Will fold for aye in the orange bowers.

That a remnant scant of the broken band
Will come again from the sunny land,
With flaming cheeks and flaming eye,
Back with the roses. Back to die.

Where marble columns, slender and high,
Like fingers point to the winter sky,
There the winter snow is drifting o'er
My bird of passage never more.

With the wings of fear from the hand of fate,
Will he fly in dread, early or late;
For year after year, while the ages last,
As year after year through the ages past,

Betwixt his grave and the midnight sky
The birds of passage their pathway high,
From the orange bowers to the arctic snow
Will screaming come and screaming go.

WHEN WILLIE'S FORIVER AWA.

In Scotch Irish Dialect.

Leddy, me leddy, it niver c'uld be,
That I c'uld wed you or you c uld wed me;
Puir Willie maun love ye but love ye in vain,
And ye maun forget and be happy again
When Willie's foriver awa, awa,
When Willie's foriver awa.

Yere father's a Laird and the proodest o' men,
Hoo he scorns us poor folk, me leddy, ye ken,

Did he ken that I loved ye, he'd ask for nae law,
He'd bang me aboon yere hie castle's hie wa',
Aboon yere ain casement I'd dance in the win'
While ye at yere leisure c'uld greet yersel' blin'
For Willie foriver awa, awa,
For Willie foriver awa.

But dinna ye greet, fair leddy and sweet,
There s plenty o' Lairds tae fa' doon at yere feet,
Their siller and lan' and their castles sae gran'
They'll gie for yere heart, they'll gie for yere han'
When Willie's foriver awa, awa,
When Willie's foriver awa.

Sae I'll e'en tae the wars wi' the comin' o' spring,
I'll fight for my country and fa' for my king,
And if some foreign lan' wi' my heart's blood be weet
What naebody kens 'ill gar naebody greet
When Willie's foriver awa, awa,
When Willie's foriver awa.

HAGAR AND ISHMAEL.

I stood by her dying bed.
"'Tis all mockery," she said:—
"These jewels that shine
On these wasted hands of mine;
They are but the token
Of vows long broken.

"Would I were dead.
How my poor heart has bled
Through long weary years,
Keeping back the burning tears,
Lest the watching world should know
Of the wretchedness below
The jewels that shine,
O'er this broken heart of mine."

I stood by her grave.
The summer air was all perfume
Of the roses all in bloom,
They w re twined in toils of grace
Round her wasted, patient face,
With its look of despair
Still lingering there.

Poor, dead wife.
How sorrowful the tale
Of the Hagar and Ishmael
Did supplant her in her home.
And, oh! agony unknown,
In his heart once all her own.
Alack! Was it not enough
That in her wounded love and pride
Often over she had died.

Why this bitter irony
Of untoward destiny?
For Hagar weeping loud
Came and kissed her in her shroud,
And exulting went her way
She is his jeweled wife to-day.

THE CAPTIVE.

Go, birdie, go.
I hinder not.
In field or grove a happier lot
Be yours, when I am all forgot.
Go and be free.
The winds are free.
So are the waves of the wide sen,
Then why should you a captive be,
Birdie?
Because, alack, you sing to me,
And in my greedy selfishness,
I care not for the sore distress
Of captivity's dire loneliness.
Ah, woe is me.
You suffer not alone. The pain
Of aching, dull despair in my poor brain,
'Tis beating like a catapult, in vain, in vain.

Oh, me.
If I could fly like you from my captivity;
Could break the chains no mortal eye can see;
Alack, I forged them, for eternity.
                    And, alack, that it is true,
Even if I had the wings I could not fly with you.
When justice scourges, 'tis unsparingly,
I get my own again and eke with usury.
                    For the wrongs I do,
And most of all to such as you,
The helpless and defenceless. What we brew
Is what we drink. Farewell to you.
                    There is the open sky,
'Tis limitless, spread you your wings and fly.
Freedom is bliss, 'tis yours, Good-bye.

AT LAST.

Have I won at last?
Are the toilsome years
    All behind, all past?

Have these dreary years
And their dark pathway,
    Led to success and victory?

And are you worth my toil,
Are you worth my care,
    My Laurel crown?

If the sun do shine and the skies be fair,
Say will you last, say will you wear,
    Till my day be done?

I fear you will sink out of sight, out of mind,
Into the darkness that lies behind
    And spreads before
Away beyond reach of human ken,
    Into evermore.

MY SHIP.

"How many watchers in life there be
For the ships that never come over the sea."
                    Mrs. Chamberlain.

I stand to-night on the silent shore,
No sail in sight on the sea before
My aching eyes. But the waves roll in
With a sob like a sigh. Their ripples fling
Brown, mouldering fragments at my feet
That the winds and the waves have ground and beat
Almost to chaff of mast and deck.
Of my own good ship, is this the wreck?
My own good ship since it sailed away;
My brow has wrinkled, my hair turned grey,
Yet I watch and wait by the silent sea
For the ship will never come back to me.

I'M DYING, EGYPT, DYING.

I'm dying, Egypt, dying,
    Through death's twilight gloom I see
Jove's own hand in far Elysium
    Close its gates on Anthony.

Close his soul that darkly hovers,
    'Twixt eternity and time,
Into Pluto's fierce, infernal
    Recompense of life-long crime.

Poised betwixt its sulphurous shadows
    And the light of elysian day,
My soul travails in retrospection
    Ere it sink eternally.

Basest treasons, foulest murders,
    Pour unstayed their tidal flood;
Total sum of the existence
    Ebbing slowly with my blood.

But no remorse, no late repentance,
    Stirs the soul of Anthony.
I would cast away Olympus
    As I cast the world away,

For the eyes she bent upon me,
    All the glory in their light,
That is bending over Egypt
    On this tranquil summer night.

For her face of matchless beauty,
    For her form of matchless mold,
I would barter all Elysium
    As I bartered Roman gold.
For the "toil of grace" that bound me,
    In its strong, unyielding chain,
What to me was earth, Elysium,
    If I wore its links in vain?

But I did not wear them vainly,
    Earth's imperial diadem,
Regal, peerless Cleopatra
    Bound her soul to mine with them.
Forfeited her life, her sceptre,
    Egypt's throne and crown for me;
Over styx dark, silent river
    She awaits for Anthony.

Dauntless in her royal beauty,
    Dauntless in her queenly grace;
Fearless of the fearful future
    That I almost shrink to face;
Cast her lot without a shudder,
    Linked her fate to mine and me,
In the dire Cimmerian darkness
    Closing over Anthony.

Closing o'er the proud triumvir,
    Dying yet with dying breath,
Jove's omnipotence deriding,
    Hurls defiance back in death.

Strike! for vengeance, all Olympus,
    Earth and Egypt each implores.
Strike! the culprit is immortal
    And eternity is yours.

Strike! I can, I do defy you;
    My Elysium mine will be;
In your despite where Cleopatra
    Waits for coming Anthony.

A PARTING GIFT.

This withered rosebud, lady fair,
    This mouldering, crumbling thing,
Do tender recollections to
    Its faded petals cling?

Is it the one last link that binds
    The present to past years;
This voiceless monitor that blinds
    Your eyes with burning tears?

Ah! yes, it was his parting gift;—
    He went to gather gold for you.
Alas! a fearful pestilence
    Was travelling westward, too.

Nay, weep not, let oblivion's wave
    Over the dead past flow;
Somewhere on his lonely grave
    The prairie roses blow.

When last spring's breezes fanned your cheeks,
    They lit a hectic flame,
A strange light to your sunken eyes
    With its first sweet flowers came.

When the withered autumn leaves
    Drop lifeless from each tree,
Lady, to the gay courts of Heaven
    He'll gladly welcome thee.

LADY ELLICE.

(Partly an old ballad.)

Lady Ellice stood under her trysting tree,
  Frantic with anger and jealousy;
Her parrot sat on the topmost limb,
  And besought her piteously.

"Oh! Lady Ellice, for Christ's sake—
  For God's sake—relent;
If your lover be false yet murder him not;
  Some day, he may repent."

"Hear you me, come down," said she,
  "Too chill is the evening air;
How came you here? Come down, sweet dear,
  You'll be chilled to death up there."

But a gay young man stepped o'er the stile
  And stood by the lady's side;
And embraced and kissed her, saying, "Ah!
  How fair is my sweet young bride.

"When we come again to our trysting tree
  She will be my own sweet wife;
And hand in hand, as heart to heart,
  We will journey down through life."

A glint of steel, and he sank to earth—
  He was dead without moan or sigh;
And with dripping hands and dripping blade
  She stood calmly by.

"Oh! God," cried the parrot, high in the tree;
  "Fly, lady, do not bide."
"Come down, come down, pretty Polly," said she,
  "Too chill is the evening tide.

"Come down, come quick, pretty Polly," she cried;
  "Pretty Polly, come down to me
And I will give you a silver beaten cage
  With a door of ivory."

"Oh, you can keep your silver beaten cage,
  And I will keep my.tree;
For she who could murder her own true love
  Would surely murder me."

"Oh, if I had my bent bow and arrow
  Well fixed upon a string,
I'd send a dart would cleave your heart
  Among the leaves so green."

"And if you had your bent bow and arrow
  Well fixed upon a string,
My feathers would carry my flesh away,
  From among the leaves so green." •

And he spread his wings and he flew away
  Screaming with might and main,
"Look, look under their trysting tree!
  Her lover she has slain."

And they found him there in the dim twilight,
  And the dagger by his side;
And they carried him to the altar's steps—
  Where waited his white-robed bride.

And a godly priest and goodly feast,
  And a lordly companie;
With Lady Ellice, all were there,
  And the parrot high in a tree.

And the parrot called to the godly priest
  And the lordly companie,
"If you look at my lady's snow-white hands,
  Blood on her hands you'll see.

"And the blood is his and the dagger hers
  Who swore in her jealous hate
She would sink it deep in his fickle heart
  Whatever might be her fate.

"And she promised me a silver beaten cage,
  With a door of ivory;
But she who could murder her own true love
  Would surely murder me."

They bind her fast and to prison haste
  Down the road past their trysting tree;
The parrot sat on the topmost limb
  And cried, "Farewell, lady."

And a Judge stood up in a Court one day:—
  "Woman, stand up," said he;
"You must be hanged by the neck till dead:
  On your soul God's mercy be."

And they made her grave in a potter's field;
  No stone or cross is there.
Of jealousy and a parrot's tongue
  Let all the world beware.

FROG AND EAGLE.

    He was seated on a log—
High and dry. The biggest frog
I'll bet you've seen this many a day.
The summer sunshine came that way,
And made him glint like burnished gold.
    Said he, "I'm gorgeous to behold.
I don't beleive in all this bog,
There is such another frog."

    An eagle resting high,
On a cloud rift in the sky,
Marked him with unerring eye,
And dropped at once upon the log
To contemplate him. And the frog
    Vented his bitter indiguation
At such presumption, in this oration:

    "Brazen thing,
Do you know I am a king?
You desecrate this sunny log
That I make my throne. This bog
Is my kingdom. Lift your feet,
They are pollution. Come, retreat,
Pack yourself and save the life,
You will lose by farther strife."

    Said the eagle all amaze;
"Well, this is the latest phase
Of the silly kingcraft craze.
You may be king, or may be none,
To my crop it is all one,
For I gobble every frog
I catch seated on a log.

"Fatter than you I never saw,
And never had a hungrier maw,"
    And he seized him then and there.
And down he went. "Well, I'll swear,"
Said the eagle. "He a king,
That's a pretty note. By jing!
But he was so good and fat,
Wish they all were kings, and sat
On the logs around like that."

And he soared light and gay
Into the sky. That's just the way
The modern trust or syndicate,
To whom the world's a world of bogs,
And all the people big, fat frogs,
Swallows early, swallows late,
Every creature comes its gate.

LADY SARA.

Lady Sara in fine array
Journeyed down the broad highway.

Of lineage long and wide estate—
Humbly a page did on her wait.

No longer young, no longer fair;
With saddened eyes and graying hair,

And stately tread, but somewhat slow—
To the town hard by would the lady go.

Sunset fire on the eastern hill—
Winter's breath in the evening's chill—

Autumn leaves that were red like gore
Carpeting the highway o'er;

A bitter wind with a dreary sigh,
Sweeping withered leaves and petals by,

Tongues of time that loudly said
Springtime and summer both had fled.

Belike the lady thought of her own
Forever and ever from her down;

For the lady sighed a dreary sigh
And dropped a tear as they drifted by.

For only this, alack, alack,
Did she turn in haste and hie her back.

Well, ah well, "The mice will play,"
Says the proverb old, "when the cat's away."

Long enough did the lady wait,
Ghostly and wan at her castle gate.

For her roystering hinds kept holiday,
But they came at last in sore dismay.

And opened it wide for her to pass,
Then closed it again, alas! alas!

When they closed her castle gate that day
They closed her castle gate for aye

On the still white lady who nevermore
Descended again from the ivied tower

Where all alone her life had passed,
Where all alone she died at last.

*   *   *   *   *   *

Oh, little page, is it anxious fears
That cause your sighs and cause your tears?

Speak, malapert, glib popinjay,
What befell our lady on that evil day?

Sure witch or warlock passed her by
And blighted her with its evil eye.

Oh, nothing our lady did befall,
Witches and warlocks be folly all.

Only a man that was bald and grey
And a lady fair passed by that way.

Nothing had they to do with blight
But my lady's face turned marble white,

And she turned to the path that homeward led
And homeward like an arrow sped.

Ye who opened the gate have said,
My lady's livid face looked dead,

As the face of her corpse will be when hid
Forever under her coffin lid.

When shrived of sin and shrived of sorrow,
She has entered Heaven's long to-morrow.

Never since then have her lips turned red,
Never since then has she looked glad,

And the whispering tongues that seldom lie,
Say that my lady is going to die.

That none will miss her in all the land,
But the Spaniel that fondly licks her hand.

Alas, for him, and, alas, for me,
If this, indeed, is going to be.

For the open moor and the winter sky,
Will be the only home of he and I.

Down the chancel cold and grey,
Where her dust moulders away,
A marble slab since she departed
To the world's says, "Broken hearted."

IS THERE A NORTH?

Then speak, for the world is listening, Oh, ye brave;
Shall Kansas be a home for the free, or a hell for the slave?

Is there a North? shall it be told
Her patriots' sons, her freemen bold,
Hath not a hand out-stretched to save
From the tyrants' power, the trembling slave?
Hath now no tongue of fire to tell,
To every land where man may dwell,
On furthest shore and widest sea
That God made all men fetter free!

Nor hath unto oppression said,
" Back, here shall thy proud waves be stayed;"
Thou shalt not cast thy withering curse
O'er our fair land it shall not nurse
The viper vile—nor will we kiss
With fawning smile, a shame like this;
Nor will we clasp thine iron hand,
Nor bow our heads at thy command.

Is there a North? will her freemen see
Their fathers' blood-bought freehold given
To scathing blight of slavery,
And curses of offended heaven?
Say, shall its mountains proud and high,
Its prairies wide and forests wild,
Their gorgeous flowers and glowing sky
Be cursed for aye, for aye defiled?

Shall ceaseless wailings of despair,
And tears of agony and blood,
From a Paradise so wide and fair,
Be the offering to God?
Shall banded hordes of human ghouls,
Tread on its dust the rights of man,
There buy and barter human souls?
Speak out and say it, ye who can!
Duquesne Boro, May 29, 1856.

YANKEE DOODLE'S CUP OF TEA.

A century has come and gone
Since Yankee Doodle rose at dawn,
To fume and fret o'er botheration,
That filled his soul with sore vexation.
Public questions much perplexed him;
Parliament for years had taxed him
On bag and baggage the utmost shilling,
And never asked if he was willing.
When he sent his king a meek petition,
George stormed of traitors and sedition;
Gave no redress, but only—dang him!—
Threatened he forthwith would hang him.
And Mr. Doodle, sorely humbled,
O'er his morning porridge loudly grumbled:
" For thorough cussedness," said he,
" King George beats all I ever see.
Law sakes! now, but I really wonder,
Does he think I'm such a gander
He'll pick me henceforth and forever,
And ask my leave or license, never?"
And Mr. Doodle thought 'twas fearful
To lose his feathers. Almost tearful,
He gabbled, kicked and loudly bickered,
Squabbled, compromised and dickered,
Until the news came o'er the sea
Old King George had taxed the tea.

Then Mr. Doodle raged and thundered,
Like other men with pockets plundered.
" What: taxed the tea!" It almost choked him
To say the words they so provoked him—
Not that he used much tea, 'tis true;
A cup on Sunday, maybe two,
But then to tax it was a blow,
Smacked of authority. And so
He buttoned his red wammus up,
And brushed his homespun breeches down,
Said to his pony, " Come, gee up!"
And took the road to Boston town.
While jogging bravely onward, he
Indulged in this soliloquy:

"I can't believe, I don't believe,
The Lord Jehovah ever gave
With a scepter and a crown
Divine right to trample down,
To grind beneath his iron heel,
To crush beneath his hand of steel,
All humanity—if he,
Whose that crown and scepter be,
Do so think fit. Now God help me,
I can't, I don't believe such thing,
The Lord Jehovah is my King."

Boston town, when he got there,
Was wrath and fury everywhere.
They'd sink the nation in the sea
Before they'd drink King George's tea;
So Mr. Doodle and his freres,
With faces blacked and smothered jeers
By the night's still darkness hid;
But history tells us what they did,
Though not what Yankee Doodle said.
For Mr. Doodle said, said he,
"Boston harbor, here is tea!
You can make it leisurely,
Draw it with the winds and tide.
In the ocean's cup—'tis deep and wide—
Will hold it well, will hold it long,
Whether it be weak or strong.
And if upon the other shore
A rampant lion fiercely roar,
Louder than the ocean wave
When tempest lashed, louder rave
Of unsparing vengeance; wildly flaunt
A battle flag; and jeering vaunt
Of the armed legions wherewith he
Can sweep the land and sweep the sea
Of treason's traitors: sweep so bare,
With fire and sword, that never there
One broken fragment's tattered shred
Will tell the living of the dead:—
Then, ocean, lift you tempest's voice,
Thunder-toned, and for us say
To his indignant Majesty:
'Poor Yankee Doodle, paltry knave,
Has scarce bare ground to dig his grave,
Between the unbroken wilderness,
Red with ferocious savages,
And the ocean's surf, before which he
Struts like your furious Majesty.
And roars as loud, and swears your tea
Shall turn the ocean's brine to gall
For you and your armed legions all
To drink or drown in! Without fail,
With leaden rain and iron hail,
And fire and sword he'll face each foe,
And lay his proud oppressor low.
Chaff of the thrashing floor shall be
His kith and kindred all, ere he
Or they shall be the slaves
Of kingcraft. In their bloody graves,
If not on earth, they can be free;
And loud he shouts for liberty,
And vows Jehovah is his king.
——Your Majesty, the forests ring
From end to end, from sea to sea,
With his seditious blasphemy.' "

This bitter message o'er the main
The tempest carried. Not in vain.
Fearful as an earthquake's shock
Soon dashed over Plymouth Rock,
Loudly thundering, wide and far,
A tidal wave of bloody war!

Through seven long years of deadly strife,
With musket, sword and scalping knife,
Yankee Doodle in the front
Bore the battle's fiercest brunt.
Ignominious defeat
And disastrous retreat
Sorely tried his heart of oak,
But shot and shell and sulph'rous smoke
Of thundering cannon, belching death
Never shook his hope or faith
Silenced not his battle cry
"On for God and liberty!"
Wavered never day or night,

From Bunker Hill to Yorktown's Height,
Where oppression and oppressor too,
Met their final Waterloo.

Then pledge to-night his memory,
His unknown grave, his cup of tea,
Beneath the eagle's outspread wings,
While "Hail Columbia" loudly rings—
And Stars and Stripes float o'er the free
Daughters and sons of Liberty.
Millvale, April 9th, 1875.

MIDNIGHT.

1875-'76.

I stood upon the threshold wide
That, unseen, arches to divide
   Eternity and time;

It reached the countless ages through;
Was spanned by heaven's ethereal blue
   And starry depths sublime.

Midnight moments almost flown
Were to my feet the stepping stone
Between two centuries. Dying one—
   The other entering

Time's wide arena. Between a bier
And a cradle bed, that each a year
   Did to the other bring,

While loud-mouthed cannon thundering,
And clanging bells and shrieking steam,
   And a shouting multitude

Welcomed the new born to the earth
And nation, at whose lowly birth
   In the new world's desert stood

Liberty with flaming sword;
While Independence defiant, poured
   Into rebellion's cup

Freedom's wine, ruby as morn;
"Take," said he to the new born
   Nation, "Drink it up."

"My son and the son of Liberty,
Live forever, brave and free."
   Then seated him on Plymouth Rock,

Placed his hands on a musket's lock;
Placed his feet on a cannon's stock;
   Their broad-sword by his side;

Showed him the wilderness before,
Showed him the ocean brimming o'er
   With resistless tide;

And louder than voice of wind or wave,
Asked why so base as be a slave
   Or vassal held in chains.

"Independence and Liberty
Gives a continent to thee!
   Keep, defend, maintain

"With our good broad-sword and thy bravery,
Let none but God rule over thee—
   Jehovah be thy king."

A mighty hand on the threshold fell;
'Twas the hand of Time, and like a knell
   It struck the midnight hour

With its last moments suddenly,
Independence armed cap a pie,
   Stepped on the threshold wide.

A flash like the flame of countless wars,
And Liberty girt with stripes and stars
   Stood by the warriors' side,

started to demolish the landlady. He would raze the house to the ground. He'd show her such barefaced robbery wouldn't do. But out in the hall he remembered that he had undertaken a similar feat once before and got razed himself and got into the lockup besides, where, having ample time to count his expenditures as well as his money, was soon convinced that nobody had stolen his money, he not having any left to steal; and now he also remembered that upon that occasion he would have had to go to jail but that his insulted landlady paid his fine. so Don reconsidered his proposed action and fell to counting up costs since Saturday night, which was pay night. Boarding, fourteen dollars: tick at the beer hall, one dollar seventy cents; the cursed old hack, four dollars: toll, seventy-five cents; supper, one dollar and fifty cents: strawberries and cream, fifty cents; smashes, juleps, cigars for himself and five other fellows, two dollars: black-eyed little girl, fifty cents. 'Tis the last feather breaks the camel's back. This last item nearly threw Don into a fit. What kind of a little girl was that? A little girl like that should be rawhided if she ever again presented herself to him. He would never set foot in that door again. Then Don counted up twenty-five dollars from twenty-seven leaves two. Whew! and two weeks to pay night. Would time and space permit a detailed account of Don's financiering from this time forth would edify and instruct the most skillful and expert in the cash department of our "Grindwell governing machine." The masterly lying that tided him out of one straight into and through each succeeding one, not only feeding and clothing himself with the best, but entertaining himself and Sue with drives, picnics, excursions, making the summer for them both one continuous holiday and golden harvest of the fruits of other people's toil, was lying that out-heroded all belief, in fact dimmed the halo around that character in Hudibras who was "for profound and solid lying much renowned," with lying, in short, he paid everything his wages couldn't pay and Don's wages couldn't pay one-half of Don's expenditures. The summer wound up with one of the grandest picnics Don and Sue had ever known, and that picnic, for reasons your veritable historian will now set forth, may be said to be the end of Don's palmy days in our burg.

'Tis a curious fact with regard to the appliances and materials used in clinker factories that they all have a strong tendency to bust; even cold water, a bucketful of which outside of a clinker factory is usually a very harmless agency, inside of one is fearfully destructive unless carefully handled. The day following the great picnic Don's head was full of that jollification. How could he remember the busting propensities and tendencies of things around him? So he gave a bucketful of water a sudden emptying over a mass of molten clinker that busted both water and clinker. The busting scattered it and melted clinker over everybody round, Don excepted, (a fool for luck), but that the blisters of all sizes that operated like the stings of so many hornets gave the recipients of this "fire shower of ruin" enough to do, Don would have had a picnic on hand; would have waltzed him round to the same tune that a picnic that day a year ahead of him eventually did. As it was there was a grand rumpus. The workmen raged, the bosses stormed, most of all the manager (the great "I am" Don called him, swearing that he had his eyes on everything and his nose in everything other people said, that was a manager's business), as if to verify Don's opinion he was instantly on hand and expressed himself so emphatically, though not usually demonstrative, that Don knew but for the great pressure of work and the great scarcity of hands he (Don) would have lit on his head outside the high enclosure. This "jen de esprit" soured the whole establishment, especially the blistered portion of it, who always looked black at Don and hinted broadly at the expediency of hanging a few of the idiots who jeopardize other men's lives with their reckless folly, going themselves scott free of suffering, expense and loss. This was very sour for Don, indeed, so much so that all the balls, oyster suppers, fairs and revivals hardly made amends to Don; in fact, but for Sue 'twould have been insupportable. But suddenly the tension relaxed, another idiot busted another bucket of water and with worse effect, and Don's escapade was forgotten. And this brought the spring and the spring brought the summer and the summer brings picnics. So there was one on the tapis pretty soon. Don, by this time in the matter of tick, was nearly swamped. Creditors' scurvy dogs dogged him everywhere. How to keep enough money out of their clutches to meet the requirements of the picnic was taxing Don's brains to the utmost. Since the calamitous busting of the bucket of water, Don had kept a wary eye on all tools and materials entrusted to his care. The ominous look of the great "I am" on that occasion had made an impression for once on his mental caoutchouc. But his present financial dilemma was enough to obliterate even the existence of the great "I am" in both mind and memory. Lost in abstruse study of the dilemma's manifold horns, a bran-new shovel dropped at Don's heels to lie while he tried to steady his bewildered wits with a glass of beer. But it didn't lie. An ever-watchful, sticky-fingered Frittaker passed that way and the bran-new shovel clave to him. An angry altercation between Don and his boss followed. The ubiquitous "I am" was immediately on hand with a face more ominous than ever. He listened and went away. Saturday was pay night. When Don, in his turn, stood at the window, the cashier, cash in hand, quietly said, "Shovels cost a dollar and half now, Mr. Frittaker." Don felt as if a valcano was lifting him off his feet, but remembering the ominous face of the great "I am," he replied in a tone of cheerful acquiescence that he knew it. The cashier counted out his wages less the price of one shovel and followed up the cash with a brief statement that henceforth the clinker factory would evolute and revolute without Mr. Frittaker's assistance. If Don a minute before felt as if a volcano was lifting him, he now felt as if two volcanoes were lifting him and an earthquake beneath them were urging them to lift. A torrent of abusive billingsgate rushed to his teeth, but somehow circumstances always "cabin crib confine" geniuses of Don's peculiar stamp. A recollection of a former experience rushed with his wrath. On that occasion he had been so

A sulphurous cloud of smoke and flame
O'er dead and dying broods the same.
And the waiting vultures perched so high,
You see no speck upon the sky?
In countless thousands, bye and bye,
To the harvest of the cannon ball
Swift as meteors will fall,
And ravening hawk and greedy crow
And wolf and wild dog. Well we know
All will be there. And they will glean
The swathes of war so white and clean
You could not tell, Heaven save the mark,
So white are the skeletons that lie
Bleaching under the open sky,
Which is the Russian or which the Turk.

Waxing crescent or waning cross.
This moral is taught the world and us.
The vultures fatten on the losers' loss
And the gainers' gain. But I forgot
That Hassan's story this is not.

Hassan dwelt on a grassy plain
Beyond the desert. On Selim's mane
A caressing hand he fondly laid
While this to Selim he softly said:
"Selim, my Selim, the Christian dog,
Detested infidel, whets his sword
'Gainst sacred Islam. Allah, Lord,
The vile bibber of unholy wine,
Devourer of the flesh of swine,
Beastly, abominable Giour,
In what age or day or hour
Hath not he the mosque profaned;
Hath not he the harem stained
With ravage, pillage, fire and sword
Whene'er victorious. Avenge us, Lord,
God of all Gods, in this holy war,
Steel each sword and scimitar
With hate and vengeance. And, Lord, be riven
The infidel's host. The winds of Heaven
Scatter like dust in the day of his flight
From the face of the earth the last trace of his might,
And the utmost border of his land
Be hot and bare as the desert's sand
When Islam and the vulture's maw
And the wild dog's ravening jaw
Have passed over it, like the breath
Of the dire Sirocco, leaving only death,
Skeletons white and ashes grey
Reaching from dawn to the close of day.
The dastard dog! The infidel!
Allah el Allah. My Selim, well,
The desert waits us, and Islam's host
Is on its border. When we have crossed
Your fairest speed, my Selim, boast.
And swift as the wind be the flight of that speed.
Of the sword of your master, the prophet hath need."

The only life where all was dead
Across the burning, sandy plain
Sans saddle, bridle, girth or rein
Our wild Mazeppa sped.
Arrow of vengeance barbed with hate,
Frenzied zeal like the hand of fate,
Urged him on with bated breath
To the carnival of death.
Not an instant Selim quailed,
Or his master, completely mailed
With an impervious panoply
Of fierce, unsparing bigotry,
Steeled heart and soul to woe or bliss,
He left his wife without a kiss,
His mother without a sigh,
To his bronze baby, no good-bye;
From his boy Hassan at his play
Without a tear he turned away,
"God and the prophet called," he said:—
His life was theirs, and theirs the blade
His fingers clenched, and both were made
To wreak God's vengeance on God's foes.
Allah el Allah, heavy blows,
And deadly thrusts should loudly tell
In numbers of the infidel.
That he had served life's purpose well.
And forth he sped across the sand,

Glowed like the flame of a burning brand.
No waving grasses by the wayside grow,
No spreading branches cool shadows throw,
Never a drop of morning dew,
Nor song of bird the ages through;
The desert highroad ever knew.
Only "ships of the desert stranded lie"
On the sandy hillocks they flit by.
He who left his mother without a sigh,
His wife without a kiss,
Our Hassan, did he care for this?
No; steed and rider, twin like twain
Across the desert swept amain,
Through torrid air that nothing stirred,
But the sand-dust cloud that blurred
Selim's shadow and his own,
That was all, and that alone.
Passed with them the sphinx by,
She who watched with sleepless eye,
Tireless, ceaseless, vigil kept
O'er the ages while they swept,
(Sweeping with the fierce cyclone)
Mountains of oblivion.
O'er wretched millions' unpaid toil
O'er vaunting triumph's richest spoil,
Over artist skill and lore,
Over bygone literature,
Painted well on marble walls,
Graven deep on granite halls,
Finite omnipotence had built
For eternity and dwelt
There, enthroned in regal state
And lawless empire o'er the fate
Of the world crouched at his feet.
"For I am God," he said. Alack!
World-wide empire, where is your wreck?
Overwhelming tides of dust
Entombed his power and pride,
His lowliest slave beside,
Crown, throne and empire lost.
To-day the wandering Arabs dwell
Above the highest pinnacle
Of Egypt's glory. Free they rove
Upon the sand drifts piled above
Imperial Egypt. Egypt lost
In the impenetrable gloom
Of earth's inevitable doom,
Nothingness at last.

Hassan saw or knew it not,
Of it Hassan never thought,
Passed the pyramids sublime;
That alone had cancelled time,
And the wreck of ages by.
With a cold, impassive eye,
With the rigid, stony stare
Of the sphinx o'er the glare
Of the desert, Hassan saw
White-winged sails from sea to sea
Bearing many an argosy;
Through the rift that cleft in twain
(When Lesseps gave the orient
In marriage to the occident)
Two continents from main to main.
On he sped upon his way,
Sped by night and sped by day,
Soon a blank of desert lay
Behind him, and before
Billows on billows, o'er and o'er,
Rolled to the Bosphorous.
A ship was on the strand, and loose
Her sails, for she was leaving—
Even then her anchor heaving,
And he and Selim sailed away
Forever! Yes, for aye.
He turned to look once more. Behold!
Across the desert's yellow gold
Dotting all the horizon
Were hundreds riding down,
Rode as he his Selim rode
For their country, prophet, God.

*   *   *   *   *   *

'Twas evening! O'er a grassy plain
Selim sped with might and main

Past marching ranks of cavalry,
('Twas Selim's fleetest passed them by)
Their crescent standards all aflame
With sunset fire. On they came.
Behind battalions thundering down
Toward the far-off horizon,
Where battle lightnings lurid flashed
Its thunder against thunder crashed.
"On, my Selim!" Hassan said.
And, shouting vengeance, drew his blade,
Rushed into the thickest fray
Of blood and slaughter. Selim's neigh
Sounded like a clarion shrill.
Echoing Hassan's savage yell.
Savage Cossacks, fierce and tall,
Faced them like a rampart's wall.
Allah el Allah! God is God!
There in torrents gushed the blood
Dripped from Hassan's streaming sword,
Dripped from Selim's reeking mane,
From many a deep and deadly gash,
The strong arm's well-directed slash,
Of foes by Hassan slain.
Selim reeled as if to fall,
Rallied, charged again the wall.
Breached it! Steed and rider fell!
Hassan to the girdle cleft in twain,
A sabre slash through Selim's brain.
Allah el Allah! It is meet,
Selim at his master's feet
Where the shock of battle spent
Its utmost fury. Where the rent,
Blood dripping banners of bigotry,
Turk or Russian won the day
Somewhere. Was it Plevna, say?

illvale Boro., September, 1877.

FAIR ELLEN AND THE BROWN GIRL.

Lord Thomas stood by his father's side
  On the towers of their castle grand,
And looked o'er the country far and wide,
  And theirs was that goodly land.

Theirs the cottages far and wide
  And many a stately hall,
And the town that reached to the river side
  With even its moat and wall.

Villages many and many a mine,
  And ships that come and go.
And flocks and herds and goodly gear—
  Their wealth did no man know.

"And now, my son," the father said,
  "This wealth will all be thine,
And thou must choose a wife whose wealth
  And rank will equal thine.

"Yon gibbet on our topmost tower
  Our lowest donjon keep
Are for our mortal foes, but yet
  My only son will eke

"Be feeding for the carrion crow,
  Or for our donjons hideous years
Black silent ages, far below
  The reach of human ears,

"If he would bate one tittle of
  My pomp and power and pride
And seek among inferiors born
  To woo and win a bride.

"Lord Douglas hath a nut-brown maid
  With more than regal mien,
And more her dower in gold and land
  Would well befit a queen.

"And more than well it doth befit
  My only son and heir
To see in Lady Maud his mate
  And future wife in her."

"Alack, my father, for I love
  Fair Elinor more than well,

And she hath lineage good and grace
  And beauty. Do not tell

"Me that I may not wed the love
  That is my life's delight,
I rather would your gallows or
  Your donjons darkest night.

"And you do know, dear father," he said,
  "How fair are fair Elinor's hands."
"I only know, my son," he said,
  "She has no other lands."

And down from those high battlements
  Lord Thomas sighing came
To seek his mother. Ill he knew
  That proud and haughty dame.

"The daughter of the Douglas proud
  My father wills I wed.
How well I love fair Elinor,
  You know, dear mother," he said.

"And, well you know, dear mother," he said,
  "How fair is sweet Elinor's face."
"And well I know, dear son," she said,
  "She has no other grace.

"The brown girl she has house and lands,
  Fair Elinor she has none.
I, too, so will and do command.
  Bring me the brown girl home."

Lord Thomas he mounted his milk-white steed
  At the dawning of the day.
Lord Thomas he put spurs to his speed
  And rode in haste away.

Like a ghostly courier fast and far
  He flitted o'er dale and down.
"Is it tidings you bring of peace or war?"
  They asked at each tower and town.

But he answered not, but rode like one
  Was riding for his life.
He flies, said they, from the headsman's axe
  Belike he has killed his wife.

And he, alack, he loved but her
  Could never be his wife.
And thought but of the fair, sweet face
  Would haunt him all his life.

With the rising sun of another day
  He reined in his milk-white steed
At the portal of an ivied tower,
  And if his heart did bleed.

None so ready as Elinor's self
  To let Lord Thomas in.
"Speak, what are the tidings of weal or woe
  To Elinor you bring?"

Oh, ghastly and wan grew the young Lord's face,
  Her's white as her marble hall.
"I come to bid you to my wedding,
  Fair Elinor; that is all."

"And if you bid me to your wedding,
  That's woe enough for me.
Make haste, depart, Lord Thomas," she said.
  "In haste I follow thee."

Lord Thomas he bowed to the Lady fair,
  And mounted his milk-white steed,
And with the haste that he came there,
  Returned with the selfsame speed.

And Elinor hied to her mother's home,
  "For thy blessing I have come.
I'm bid to Lord Thomas' wedding, and
  In haste would fain be gone."

"Few will be your friends, my child,
  The bride's your mortal foe,

For your own sake, my daughter, be wise,
To Lord Thomas' wedding don't go."

"I care not that I friends do lack,
I fear no mortal foe,
Be it for life or be it for death
To Lord Thomas' wedding I'll go."

She dressed herself in scarlet red,
Her waiting maids in green,
And every town that they rode by
They took her to be some queen.

And when they came to Lord Thomas' castle
The walls with mirth did ring,
Yet who so ready as Lord Thomas himself
To let fair Elinor in?

He took her by her lily-white hand,
He led her up the hall
Where regal in jeweled grandeur sat
The bride and the nobles all.

"The fairest lady in all the land
Has come to our feast" said he.
"The woman I love best in all the world,
Warm let her welcome be."

The brown bride's face grew black with rage,
With hatred and with scorn.
"Do you flaunt me with your paramour?
Would God I had ne'er been born."

"There is a well in her father's garden.
It is all under a tree.
Not purer than his Elinor's self
Its crystal waters be.

"You are my wife, I do command,
Unbend that frowning brow
And kiss her whom a prince might kiss
Or eke our sovereign bow.

"Nay, God, what is it, my Elinor!
Alack! Oh, woe betide,
Her dagger in your heart. The fiend
Is with your heart's blood dyed.

"Oh, speak! One parting kiss, one glance.
What, not one last good-bye,
And in my arms and on my breast
So bloodily to die."

He laid her softly, gently down.
She looked like peaceful sleep.
Too horror stricken everyone
To either speak or weep.

And turning to his scowling bride,
Said, "Wife, we will not mourn,
But we will hasten after her
Who never can return."

From brow to chin her frowning face
Fell like a flash in twain.
His sword dripped gore from hilt to point.
She never breathed again.

He placed the hilt against the floor,
The point against his breast,
And these three lovers evermore,
God grant their souls find rest.

And horror seized that festive throng,
They fled in sore dismay.
As humbly as the humblest hinds
In their haste that evil day.

But Douglas, vowing vengeance dire,
Took up the hapless bride.
"Poor daughter, dead. Your funeral pyre
Shall light the world, and wide

O'er land and sea, the ashes rain,
And smoke and cinders fly

When this old castle in a cloud
Of ruin storms the sky."

And he made good his fearful threat.
Like ravens on the wing
There came on every flowing tide
The ships that brought them in.

From o'er the sea, wild savages,
They camped upon the coast,
They swarmed like locusts and devoured
All things, that ravening host.

A funeral pyre. Yea, God. By night
It did eclipse the moon,
The stars went out in the lurid light,
By day eclipsed the sun.

Cottage and hall and tower and town,
Lit as with lightning's stroke.
In the fiery maelstorm vanished all,
In ashes, dust and smoke.

And he who built that castle old
Had said it would defy
The storming of the centuries
Through all eternity.

Yet ramparts, towers and parapets
Seethed like destruction's leaven
Beneath the cannon balls that struck
Like thunderbolts from Heaven.

Ruthless destruction faced at last
Blank waste of land and sky,
And from the famine stricken coast
Were fain in turn to fly.

These the savage human wolves,
Gathered from wood and wold,
With nothing human in their breasts
But greed of spoils and gold.

They spread their canvas wide and white,
The winds blew out to sea.
When in the moon's weird, waning light,
Think what their terrors be.

For high the vanished towers again
Spring up like shafts of light,
And all their battlements are manned
By spectres gaunt and white.

And banners like white winding sheets
Float o'er the ghostly walls,
And ghostlier still a spectral host
Dance through those spectral halls.

And eke as struck the midnight hour
Behold a bridal train
Steps lightly through the phantom walls
To the festal board again.

Again Lord Thomas clad in mail
Gleams like the moon's wan light,
And leads a phantom Elinor
In a shroud, how snowy white.

Again the brown girl's face grows black,
Her jeweled dagger gleams;
Again fair Elinor sinks in death,
And red her life blood streams

Adown her winding sheet and shroud
And the brown girl's bridal robe and train;
And her bridal veil is spattered all
With the gruesome crimson rain.

Again the brown girl reels and sinks
Beside her victim fair.
Again Lord Thomas seeks in death
Refuge from love's despair.

Then shrieking all, with one accord,
The ghostly companie

Fled wildly through the spectral walls
That crumbled silently

Into the moon's pale beams again
And vanished from the earth
With all their ghostly panoply
And ghostly woe and mirth.

And they who spellbound watched that night
This orgie of the dead,
With oar and rudder sought to speed
The winds by which they fled.

Their palsied hands with trembling haste
Urged for their native coast.
Each saw the other old and grey,
A trembling, white-haired ghost.

Transformed, transmuted by that hour
Of spectral horror, every one
Grew old and grey who earthly fears
Of hell or heaven ne'er had known.

Appalling blackness swallowed up
The sky and moon and stars,
And peals of thunder shook the earth
Like the castle's falling towers.

And the tempest shrieked like the terrible cries
Of the wives and mothers slain,
And maiden and child who pleaded wild
For mercy, all in vain.

They spread all canvas to the blast,
The mountain waves they climbed.
What were the dangers gathering fast
To the horrors lay behind?

And dawn broke on a rock-bound coast,
The breakers rolling high.
Their native land was that o'er head
Amid the clouds and sky.

Brook you delay who can or may
In some dark, trying hour.
They knew none. In the darksome grey
Of earliest dawn, they did not cower.

They set each helm and each oaken prow
For their native land and the clouds and sky,
And mount on the breakers. Bravely now
In the raging surf they are stranding high.

Where the sea birds perch. where the ledges hang
O'er fathomless depth, the breakers roar,
The winds lash fiercely, they sway and swing,
But the waves urge on to the rock-bound shore.

And these fierce, free booters, grim and grey,
Do they bend their knees and thank the Lord,
And land their booty, their priceless prey,
Gathered with fire and sword.

Nay, nay. As if all sense bereft
Each to the mountains wildly fled.
Neither to the right nor the left looked he
Who was flying from the dead.

And when Lord Douglas viewed the land
From his castle's towers at eventide,
He saw them stealthily hurrying down
The rugged mountain side.

Out of the woods on the mountain's brow
Like fugitives flying in wild retreat,
And the mad disorder of those who seek
To save their lives after dire defeat.

For his castle gate sped those flying feet.
"By my halidom," said the haughty chief,
"Gabriel's trump must have called the dead
Out of their graves to the judgment seat,

"Else whence come all these grey old men?"
But they clamored loud at his castle gate.

"Oh, master, chieftian, take us in;
Judgment pursues us, we cannot wait.

"One and all that we put to the sword,
Sword in hand are in hot pursuit
Of our living souls. Open, dear lord.
Oh, open, open, for hand and foot.

"Body and soul we served you well.
We spared no creature. We slaughtered all
That had breath of life. Left no tongue to tell
One word of the past. Not even a wail

"Of tower and town. Oh, chieftain, hear
Your vassals' call. Make no delay.
We be all dead men with the deadly fear
Of the immortal souls we could not slay.

"For their souls have followed us o'er the sea.
For terror and horror look how we be
Grown grey and old. And the twilight falls
Master, we die before your walls."

And they opened the gates. They were maniacs all
And raved in wild frenzy. 'Twas a gruesome sight
For they fled in terror from hall to hall,
From the donjons keep to the battlements height.

Daytime or nighttime brought no surcease.
To reason, to menace, was all in vain.
In friends and foes they saw only ghosts,
And fled in wild terror, might and main.

And Douglas that never knew human fear,
Or human pity, or spared a foe,
Grim old savage, was powerless here
In his own stronghold to strike a blow;

For the gruesomeness of he knew not what,
That bound his hand and stayed his sword.
So he called the priests. They control, he thought,
All things infernal. We'll praise the Lord.

And they came at once with their crosses and books
And censers and wands to abjurgate
The power of Satan and all ghostly spooks,
And closed and barred the castle gate.

And Douglas they packed to the Holy land.
Crusading, they thought, would do him good.
From eternal hell fire a burning brand
Plucked just in time. He must and should

Save his precious soul by serving God
And the Holy Virgin and Holy Cross.
And they called his clansmen from mountain and
wood,
And equipped them all without further loss

Of precious time, both foot and horse.
And the maniacs down in the donjons keep,
Said the wise old Abbott, "Who could sleep
Where they are raving. And what is worse

"The holy army needs more men
Bravely accoutred. May God them speed,
For fighting the infidel Saracen
They're the very thing in our urgent need."

And a helmet on every crazy head.
They followed a floating gonfalon
That flashed like a meteor as they sped
Like the gust of a hurricane through the town

To the river side, where their waiting chief
Ruefully watched them board the ship.
Believe me well that was a trip
Surpassed the bounds of all belief.

For they climbed the masts and they climbed the
shrouds;
They perched on the sails and looked like clouds
In a stormy sky, or in shrieking crowds
They fought for the helm or danced on the prow,
And raced on the bulwarks, above, below,
While the air grew green and the sun turned blue;
'Twas pandemonium through and through,

From the cursing captain to the swearing crew
And frantic Douglas. Nobody knew
One moment's sleep, one instant's rest,
Or peace for aching head or breast.

Douglas thought no more of his castle grand.
He thought no more of his power and pride.
He only wished that in old Scotland
The hour he was born he had only died.

They sighted a headland in Palestine.
Captain and crew fell on their knees
And thanked the Lord. And for the first time
In all his life the Douglas crept
Away alone and sat down and wept

For sheer relief. They piped all hands
And launched the boats. 'Twas fair and fine
That day on the coast of Palestine;
But calamity comes upon all lands.

With stealthy tread, that glowing sky
And glowing sea were portents dire
Of the molten lava and Greek fire
Landed that day on the scorching dry.

Edge of the open, sandy plain,
White with the tents of the Saracen,
And the molten lava poured amain
When the raving lunatics, there and then,

Poured into that camp. If from on high
Greek fire had poured from the open sky,
The pall that instantly rose and spread
Like a midnight canopy overhead

Had not been blacker. Storks and dust,
Vultures and cormorants seethed and whirled
Like the total wreck of a ruined world
O'er the utter wreck of the encamped host.

Said the captain, "Good-bye to ye everyone.
Your like was never on land or sea.
Wherever you go 'neath the shining sun
The opposite road is the road for me."

Every tack of his canvas at once he spread.
When night closed in they were leagues away;
Yet black as ever that canopy
Hung over that camp. If all were dead

Or all were living. The cormorants
And storks and dust still filled the sky.
'Tis well to believe their former haunts
Were untenable when they perched so high.

Europe's money had all run out,
And Europe's credit just about,
At the end of ten years time
Fighting the wars in Palestine.

The stay in proceedings was all complete
When nobody had a crumb to eat.
Victory's self brought dire defeat;
The allied armies were in full retreat.

And Douglas, old and dazed and grey,
Was in the van in naked feet
And a palmer's gown that evil day
Through southern Europe's dust and heat.

To beg his way to the highland hills,
And his old stronghold, if so God wills;
And he looked like a dried up skeleton
A thousand years old if it was one.

Meanwhile, in his stronghold while he was gone,
The purgation had been a thorough one.
His wife an abbess, his daughter a nun,
And his son a priest and ambassador gone
To the Holy Pope at Holy Rome

On the road to Heaven and a good way up.
He would pretty soon get a Cardinal's hat
For his priestly ways and devotion that
Of holiest fervor was a brimming cup
Flowing o'er without let or stop.

All lusts of the flesh with the ghosts had gone;
No carnal things in his castle walls,
But holiest monks up and down its halls
Chanted their litanies one by one.

'Twas a perfect earthly paradise;
Not a drop was left of his rare old wine,
Not a grain of the gold would have filled a mine,
Not a gem of his jewels beyond all price.

Nothing was left of those carnal things
And ungodly follies. A censer swings
In every chamber, in every hall,
And cross upon cross on every wall.

And what before it had never been,
From top to bottom 'twas thoroughly clean
And full of sweet odors. Honey and cream,
Venison, pastries, rich and good,
Praying monks need substantial food.

And his grand old forests were full of deer,
And fish and game, why lack good cheer?
So one-half sat on their knees at prayers
While tother half roasted and fried down stairs.

Through all the ten years had come and gone,
With baking and boiling they never got done.
Cooking and eating under the sun
Was their only pleasure, their only fun.

They slept and rested when the day was done,
And early next morning again begun
To cook and eat. One evening late
A palmer stood at the outer gate.

A dazed and dead looking old galoot
Covered with dust from head to foot.
He said he had come from far Cathay
Through the half of Europe tramped day by day

With Coer de Lion. The dust on his cloak
And his naked feet, and hair so grey,
Thick as the grime of a century,
Proclaimed the truth of what he spoke.

So they took him round to an empty stall,
Piled plenty of straw against the wall,
Gave him plenty to eat. Said the Abbott wise,
"A creature like that is full of lice."

Not one could tell how he got away,
But the palmer was gone at break of day.
His nest in the straw against the wall
He left behind him, that was all.

And they marvelled and wondered every one,
The like of that they had never known;
And while they wondered, sure as fate,
Twelve palmers stood at the outer gate.

Hooded and cloaked from toe to chin,
Wise or unwise, they let them in.
The warder turned to shut the gate.
The palmers seized and bound him straight.

A thousand highlanders rushed within
And filled the castle far and wide
With dirt uproar and tumultuous din,
Each had a claymore at his side.

A thousand rushed in through an open door
No monk had ever seen before.
The battlements shook with their wild acclaim;
Douglas was home to his own again.

To the nethermost depths of the donjon keep
They hustled the monks that night to sleep.
They piled no straw against the wall,
Gave nothing to eat at all, at all.

But they bustled them back at the dawn of day.
The first old palmer that came that way;
The same that slept in the pile of straw,
Now as trim and as clean as a young jackdaw,
Stood before them just as grey;

But booted and spurred, and the Douglas crest
Upon his bonnet, and on the breast
Of his Douglas plaid. And he said, "By my life,

"If you don't send back my daughter and wife
And my only son, ye be all dead men,
And your abbey an ash heap. No Saracen
Was ever a rogue like you thievish pack;
All things you have stolen send them back.

"Money and jewels, gold and wine,
To the last farthing's worth, all that's mine.
You see yon gallows high on my towers,
You see this scaffold inside my gate,
Mark them well, for sure as fate,
I'll hang or behead you every one,
If you disobey me. Now, begone."

They did his bidding without delay.
They reached the abbey about midday;
With hunger and terror and want of sleep,
They were almost dead. Could only weep.

But, praise the Lord, there was still a cask
Of the Douglas wine in the abbey s keep,
And baking had been the morning's task,
Fresh venison pies and many a heap

Of bannocks and cookies; and the brethren spread
The midday board with a plentitude,
Filled every stomach and settled each head,
And fell to the brim they went to bed.

And rose next morning for consultation,
And vented their burning indignation.
They, the holiest, best of men,
Berated as worse than the Saracen.

And the wise old abbot, with sobs and tears,
Told how they had toiled for him all the years,
Tilled his fields and tended his fold
Cleaned his fortress, filthy and old.

And his savage son and inhuman wife
And barbarous daughter, had tamed all through
And civilized with enough to do;
Had changed their very nature and life.

And this was their recompense, braw and fine.
And so all round they took more wine
To brace them up. Without let or stop
They ransacked the abbey from bottom to top.

Soon they had loaded a caravan
With the Lord knows what. On every hand
Costly plate and garniture.
They had brought it home to keep secure

And safe for him whatever time
He got back from the wars in Palestine;
And all his gold and cash for the wine
Packed all together, lost no time.

They knew the Douglas and his ways
And the wretched folly of unwise delays,
And as to sacredness of abbess or nun,
No use of talking, both went home,
So impotent was bankrupt Rome
Nothing could be said or done.
So all their jewelry went along
For the barbarous splendors of the old days.
No doubt they'd forsake the new, godly ways,
So they washed their hands of both abbess and nun
And sent a courier post haste to Rome
And a letter with him setting forth
Their days were numbered on this earth
If the young Lord Douglas didn't come home.

With the utmost speed wouldn't break his neck,
Our lives are the forfeit, hurry him back,
And all saints and all angels everywhere
Guard the road he comes with the greatest care.

Surely Lord Douglas was crazy mad;
His doings were awfully, horribly bad.
Every saint and virgin he could find
And censer and cross the monk left behind

That was gold or silver, the ungodly Scot
Melted at once in a smelting pot;
Into shillings and guineas coined the whole lot,
Nor with this sacrilege did he stop.

Every sacred thing wasn't silver or gold
He fired it out of his old stronghold;
Filled moat and ditch with the awful wreck
Of shrines, crosses and altars, beads a peck;

And then went up to his battlements
And relieved his mind with these comments:
"Made my wife an abbess, my daughter a nun,
And a drivelling priest of my only son.
"Stole my money and swilled my wine
While I was fighting in Palestine.
Until I was sent up to Cathay
Or somewhere near it, many a day
A prisoner to the Saracen,
Than whom there never were better men.
They are everything good that we are not,
Pope, priest or cardinal or Scot.

"Have a civilization we do not know,
Would be perfection, but here below
There's always a hitch, some kind of deadlock.
They've got a Koran, just like the stock

"Of Bibles rotting in the ditch,
Would God I could sweep the world of such."
And up he got and went down stairs,
And finding his abbess and nun at prayers

Dispatched his gillies all through the land
With invitations on every hand
To every youthful cavalier,
Prince, Duke or Earl, far and near.

To his abbess and nun right away
Announced they should have a gala day,
And emptied every old oaken chest
Of all their fardingales. Their richest, best

Silks, velvets, laces, jewels rare,
For bosom, girdle, neck and hair.
And said, "Dear daughter, your best now wear,
The flower of the land will all be here,

"Maiden, wife and cavalier.
And choose you a sweetheart, whate'er he be,
Rich or poor, he shall please me
If he pleases you, your happiness.

"Think of it, daughter, first and last,
Choose you wisely and choose you well,
Of all the King's knights pick the flower.
They will all be here in another hour.

"Your poor, dead sister repenteth me,
Sold like her you shall never be."
And all the King's knights gathered in,
Came like the sunshine and the wind.

Frolicking, laughing, true as the steel,
In their burnished armor. Who could feel
Like a drooling nun in such company?
The nun departed, went to stay.

As was his custom, the old Lord went
In the evening late to his battlements;
That night with the moonlight they were all aglow
Everything sparkled like frozen snow.

On the shiniest side of a snow-white tower,
Sat a belted knight. One of the flower
Of England's knighthood—rich and grand—
Percy, Duke of Northumberland.

And his own fair daughter, they saw him not,
They were spooning moonshine out of a cup,
And each was greedily drinking it up.
Thought the old Chief as he stole away,
Oh, happy hour ! Oh, lucky day !
And he told his wife, and in ecstacy
She clapped her hands, and the rest of her life
The abbess was lost in the mother and wife.

When it rains luck it always pours,
Young Lord Douglas stood out of doors
Wondering much at the revelry,
For an abbess and nun such company
Was hardly fitting. And his cowl and gown
Were meant for a cloister; dark his frown,
But father and mother were wild with joy,
To have him back, their only boy;
And his mother adjured him when alone
To speak no word about abbess or nun;
Your father 's a madman about the matter,
The less that is said, dear, all the better;—
And old Lord Douglas came that way,
And prompt as ever said his say.
"My son, 'tis now the time of life
You choose yourself a fitting wife;
Here's pick and choice within our gate,
No better time to choose a mate.

"Think not of our lineage, wealth and pride,
There is love that is better than all three;
Choose you her who will give it thee;
Rich or poor, make her thy bride."

The young lord answered neither yea nor nay,
Looked perplexed and went his way;
But the cowl and gown vanished for aye;—
He wore a Douglas plaid that very day.

And the old Lord Douglas made the company laugh
About a prodigal son and a fatted calf;
And nobody spoke of a renegade priest,
And they all the better enjoyed the feast.

On his battlements when he got there,
Belted knights and ladies fair

Were spooning moonshine everywhere;
Most of all the renegade priest

Was dishing up the glittering feast
With laughing eyes and prodigal hand,
To the sweetest lassie in all the land;
Poor as a church mouse, but not the least

In rank and title. His dearest friend
Was Robert, Duke of Albany,—
Own brother of the king. and she
Was his fair daughter. What better end
Could come to his dearest hopes than this,
Besides the cunning, wily priests,
And their deep-laid scheme to underhand
Secure his fortress, gold and land
To the brotherhood, it brought to grief.

And smiling faces and happy looks,
Laid forever the ghostly spooks,
When on the double wedding day
Old Lord Douglas and Albany
Gave the smiling brides away
To their belted knights. And his final say
Old Lord Douglas said it then,
He learned it from the Saracen—

"Never for gold sell your love,
Never for gain barter truth;
Justice reigns in Heaven above,
Be yours its crown of immortal youth.

Let us all with one accord,
For this new doxology—
Thank the Lord.

Don Frittaker's History.

THE FRITTAKERS are a very numerous family—multitudinous, in fact. Historically, Don is the oldest, being the first to enjoy the supreme distinction of having his history written for him, and written by an historian who has every qualification to make it in every respect the best history that has ever been published or that can or will be published. "World without end, Amen."

But if Don is the oldest Frittaker historically, he is not the oldest Frittaker chronologically by a million of years or so. There is evidence that would fill two or three British museums that the Frittakers existed in force and were divided into the sticky and slippery fingered branches when the moon was greener than any green cheese you ever saw, and green with grass, and all her craters were in full blast, and her atmosphere was the correct thing and had loaded both her poles with glaciers on the most scientific principles, and on the same principles by precipitation filled all her rivers, lakes and seas brim full of water. That was a long time before Paradise materialized, and when it did the Frittakers came down from the land of Noh — and here I will only state that they came for no good for I am writing Don's history and not theirs.

Two striking peculiarities characterize the Frittaker family and divide it into the two branches to which I have already alluded.

To the fingers of one branch everything they touch sticks fast—to the fingers of the other branch nothing whatever will stick, least of all five dollar greenbacks or fractional currency.

Don belongs to the other branch.

They all say that this world owes them a living, and they all want a good fat one. And when this old world don't duff it up readily they all want other people's pockets to duff; that is, they want to square the circle of this present existence by dividing everything up all around once a year or so. If there is only enough to give fifty cents apiece all around, why, everything is square all around of course. That is their gospel, and Don's, for a fact, an authentic, incontrovertible fact. There will be no other kind of facts in this history, and I'm going to back up every fact with such veritable truths and indisputable evidence as will make Don's history a Webster's Unabridged Dictionary, a Book of Mormon and an indisputable Koran regarding Don and every Frittaker that ever has been or will be to every man, woman or child who could, should or would seek information regarding any or every Frittaker. And I'm going to write Don's history for him and gratis—for nothing—write it and not charge him a cent for it. Could or would anybody write Don's history cheaper than that? Neither could anybody be better qualified for writing Don's history. Although I say it myself it is true, I say it again that I never make any mistakes, and that is the first, last and best qualification in the world for writing history. Who wants a history with mistakes in it? A history with mistakes in it is a sheer delusion and a snare. A few errors may creep into Don's history, to err is human, and just like a woman ; "for a woman lacks originality and genius and when decked with a little brief authority (as, for instance, writing history) becomes bold, arrogant and full of folly," says an old English writer.

To begin with Don's history. When Don came to our burg and worked in our clinker factory, is time enough to begin with Don's history. To go too far back, to begin too early would overdo Don's history at the very outset, would necessitate at least two volumes of introduction. To write two volumes of introduction to a history requires a Henry Thomas Buckle, and I ain't Mr. Buckle. And this of course will bring the constitutional grumblers to the front who will say, "Poor Don Frittaker, 't would have been better for you if she had been," and then other grumblers will ask, "Why did'nt Don Frittaker write his own history, 'tis his own business," and that will make everybody very mad, and they'll all jabber together that by reason of interviewers and writers of history nobody gets a minute's peace now-a-days. That's the kind of thanks one gets when one sows universal benefac tions broadcast and writes a new bible worth a stack of old bibles. Don's first care when he came to our burg was to get a good boardinghouse, seven dollars a week, others were five and people said fair boardinghouses, too. But Don knew them under great stress of weather, Don had sought refuge in them off and on, but it took stress of weather to make him do it. You never saw a green cucumber there until they were two or three cents a piece, too long to wait in the spring by half. There is no stage in a cucumber's existence when it will refresh a fellow like the one that early in the spring costs eight or ten cents, and what holds good with regard to cucum bers holds equally good regarding tomatoes, strawberries and other luxuries of the season. Don knew it and an extra dollar or two was nothing when a fellow knew what the difference between a seven and a five dollar boarding- house really was. The seven dollar boardinghouse Don selected had a stylish front, white blinds on all the windows; a dingy mean place makes a fellow cheap and Don hated cheapness. Don's new landlady's eyes were remark- able for an expression of wakeful, watchful anxiety as if the invading host of a mighty enemy had camped around about and she were a picket forever on duty, and the haggard, broken down look of her thin, sallow features strenghtened this impression in the minds of all but Don. Don's mind knew no impressions of any kind, so great was its elasticity. The landlady wasn't a Frittaker, probably that more than anything else will account for her being forever on guard and that taken altogether she contrasted unpleasantly with the white blinds and the cheerful look of the clean, tidy house. Beside guarding the boarding house and some twenty boarders she guarded one hired girl, three children and a husband. The husband sick, always sick. Some people said 'twas the five or six dollars worth of medicine he took every week that kept him alive, other people said 'twas the five or six dollars worth of medicine every week that kept him sick, a wide difference of opinion certainly. For the poor landlady her face grew more haggard, her eyes more anxious with every passing week. Her husband was a most loving, affectionate husband and father, too, and as usual when such is the case she was sacrificing all things in a frantic effort to save him. There was no counting of dollars but an endless repetition of "Heaven, Oh Heaven above, only spare me my poor Johnny!" And this state of affairs that should have been a great comfort to the sick man was no comfort at all. He only thought, constantly thought, how in the end his poor wife must and would go under in her wild struggle for his life and kept mentally repeating over and over "would I was dead, would I was dead." So you see this was a landlady with her hands full of trouble and her heart full of sorrow, and her head full of the cares and perplexities that both trouble and sorrow furnished without stint. As might be expected, neither care nor perplexity grew smaller by degrees nor beautifully less by having Don Frittaker added to the number of her patrons. At his very first dinner Don remarked very first thing that cucumbers were remarkably early and cheap people said. "No, no," said the landlady, "they're not cheap, they're very dear, ten cents each." Was it possible, Don was astonished, only ten cents, why that time last year they were fifteen cents his landlady told him and she always had cucumbers and good ones and plenty of them. The poor landlady glanced furtively around to see how this affected the other boarders and saw with dismay that one and all of them looked as if they couldn't eat another dinner without cucumbers. Poor woman, she couldn't afford to let them wear any expression of countenance they pleased, next day there were cucumbers sliced very thin and made to cover as much plate as possible, a state of affairs Don didn't fail to illustrate with various antics holding the pieces between him and the light with a fork, lifting at them with a spoon as if they couldn't be lifted at all (Don has been doing that lately with a different kind of vittles) nevertheless taking care to spoon the biggest share into himself. Don knew when he could do such things, he also knew when he could not do them. He discovered that unexpectedly once just after his first supper in a former boarding house whereat he had diverted his new messmates with similar feats of legerdemain. Immediately after in the sitting room an immense Irishman brought forward a pair of hobnailed brogans that were simply frightful and asked Don if he saw them. Don said he didn't know how he could help seeing anything obstructing the view to that extent. "Well, they're mine," said the Irishman. "Well, I've no objections," said Don, "I'm only too glad they ain't mine, does

your feet fit them?" "Nately," said the Irishman, "and I'll tell ye young-
ster if ye show any mair o' yer'e imprunce at my table ye'll see ho'o they'll
fit you." From that day Don took particular care to inform himself whether
his prospective landlord was Irish and wore brogans or not. When Don
inquired respecting his present landlord a fellow boarder stated there was
such a cove upstairs somewhere, never saw him, was all the time sick he
believed. So the coast was clear and Don at his leisure could privateer at his
own discretion and his own discretion urged him to exert to the utmost an
almost unlimited capacity for annoying and harrassing any creature totally
at his clemency, and henceforth no oversight, no blunder, no trifling omission
escaped him. The poor landlady's confusion and mortification, even her often
humble apologies never caused him to relent for one moment but rather
intensified his satire and ridicule. The landlady had once or twice attempted
to redress her grievances with fellows of this stamp by turning them out
but the fellows who turned in were little better and went off in the end leaving
a two weeks bill unsettled. At present so pressing was her need of every
dollar she must, so long as Don paid up, tolerate his insolence, so your
historian thinks that Don for the present is domiciled in a boardinghouse
that suits him exactly; if it don't, your historian don't know what would suit
him exactly. Whether it suits him or not it is the only one the facts of
Don's history have provided for him at this juncture which shows the great
disadvantage a historian labors under when writing a history instead of a
romance, for in the romance you invent all the facts and by so doing please
everybody, whereas you must write a history with facts that are already
invented and so badly invented, too, they will please nobody, but instead will
make everybody very mad at yourself; for everybody thinks the stubbornness
of them originates in your own pigheadedness and everybody abhors pigheadedness. Suited or not suited, one fact is certain, Don applied for and
immediately received work in the clinker factory hard by; wages, two dollars
twenty-five cents per day.

As a general rule the weather in the summer months outside of the
clinker factories is rather warm; as a particular rule, inside of the clinker
factories in the summer months, it's hot as the summer breath of the Sahara.
Many devices have been tried before now for cooling the summer breath of
the clinker factories, but never with much success. Don Frittaker said they
were humbugs, every one of them, that one glass of lager beer or ale was
worth the whole lot of them, was in fact the only cooling device was worth
anything, and by taking the proper number of glasses, a fellow could regu-
late his temperature to suit himself, and the clinker factory temperature too.
So Don took many glasses, and being a whole souled fellow, always took
one or more fellows with him to the beer hall and refrigerated them at his
own expense. There was nothing cheap about that. But although this
kept his temperature natural through the week while working in the factory.
It wouldn't keep it normal on Sunday when he didn't work in the factory;
in fact, a fellow in summer must go to the country to keep normal on Sunday:

nothing like the country air if you take it in a buggy and a pretty girl takes it in the buggy along with you. Don had known all this for a long while, so having secured work and a boarding house, a pretty girl was now in order, and Don kept his eyes round pretty sharp, but as every girl in our burg was prettier than another, and every one of them had strings enough to her bow already. Don ran a smart risk of smothering in his own temperature some Sunday, when fortunately a new girl moved into our burg at this critical juncture, and she being very pretty, and having left the old strings of her bow behind, possibly because they were not worth moving, and Don getting an introduction before any other body, Don was attached to her bow at once, and it was now in order for her to tune Don to her own particular key, and make all the sweet melodies she could out of so much dissonance. Don called as early as possible to get tuned up, and his new girl received him with great suavity, and placed the easiest of easy chairs in the pleasantest possible situation for him. When Don sat down in it, a black eyed little girl sat down too with an air of great hesitation on a chair close beside him, and with the most charming naivity, told him how such a nice gentleman had called a little while before, and made her a present of a quarter-dollar. Don produced his pocket book, and gave her a twenty-five cent script, the blackeyed little girl clasped her hands in an ecstacy of delight and exclaimed! Oh what a nice gentleman you are, Oh thank you, thank you, and slid down off the chair and disappeared, and his new girl (her name was Susan Frittaker, black-eyed Susan, Don always called her,) chatted merrily all the time, and apparently neither saw nor heard the black-eyed apparition, but descanted on the delights of the country, these delightful summer days, especially a Sunday drive. Don chimed in, he felt on this particular subject, all that any body, even Susan, could feel such a drive was the one indispensable necessity of a clinker factory fellow's life, in summer his temporal well-being depended upon it wholly, solely, and as Sue saw the matter in exactly the same light, he at once proposed that she should share the benefits and advantages of a drive the following Sunday, which was to be sure, but a meet and fitting reward of so much good sense and sound judgment. Sue graciously accepted the graceful tribute to her merit, and told him of a charming hotel that a number of the elite patronized, how super excellent the dinners and suppers were, and how fortunate it was the strawberry season was just coming in. Don's delight was unbounded; was it any wonder, fresh fields and pastures new, beautiful girl and strawberries, too. On Sunday Don was promptly on hand with the most stylish rig he had been able to procure. Susan went to get her hat and Don sat down in the easy chair, and instantly the black-eyed little girl fluttered to his side and sat down, too, and forthwith told him what a comfort and delight that twenty-five cents had been to her, and that if it had only been fifty cents, she could not have spent it all whereat Don laughed as if it was the best joke in the world, produced his pocket-book and a fifty cent greenback, answering her that a quarter would'nt buy much these hard times, he knew himself. The black eyed little girl eagerly grasped the money, repeated the former pantomime and disappeared, her father, mother and three brothers seemingly wholly oblivious of her entrance, actions or disappearance. Sue now entered in a new summer suit so fashionable, rich and stylish, and looked so charming that Don pronounced her the loveliest girl he had ever seen. If there was any cheap thing in life Don detested more than another, it was a homely, ill dressed girl. The one chief aim of Don's life was to shine upon such occasions as Sunday drives, picnics, and balls. To shine on such occasions with an ugly, unfashionably dressed girl was out of the question, you couldn't attract attention, you caused no envy. There was no sensation when you came in, no flutter when you went out; in short, it made a fellow cheap, cheap. Don never patronized homely girls, would as soon have toted out his grandmother or any old maid, or any of Barnum's stock.

If Sue was lovely in Don's eyes, she was more than lovely in her own, and didn't conceal the fact, but rather made free display of her conviction. The circle she moved in took girls at their own valuation, therefore self-assertion in her case was meritorious, and as it consisted mostly in bad grammar, and disdainful airs and vulgar slang, it didn't cost much, and could be used freely, and Sue used it freely, and received consequently the hearty admiration of the beaux, and the equally hearty detestation of the belles, and it would be hard to say which she prized most highly.

When a fellow has a divinity like this by his side it's impertively necessary that he should make the dust fly. A horse hired for four dollars won't make the dust fly, unless you make the whip fly pretty lively. So Don made the whip and the dust both fly.

They hadn't been long on the road, when a two-forty nag, a fast young sport and equally fast girl overtook and passed them despite of Don plying the whip to the utmost. Drive, drive urged Sue, and Don drove, drove till the dripping back of the four-dollar horse grew foamy under the harness. "The infernal old hack," said Don, "I'll kill him if he don't keep up," and the miserable hack seemed to know the danger, and exerted sinew, nerve and muscle to the utmost, but in vain, and to the intense mortification of Don and Sue he fell behind, and the young sport and his gay companion turned. The sport bowed with a derisive ha, ha, ha! and the feminine loveliness kissed her hand and waived back the kiss with an equally derisive he, he, he. Could mockery go farther? Don was frantic and Sue was frantic and the wretched hack. Well, oh, well, "The mills of God grind very slow, but grind exceeding sure."

"Curse the devilish brute," said Don, "for a cent I'd tie him up and lash him to death." "Would serve him right," said his gentle companion, whose fine new suit was turning gray as ashes with dust. Don kept the reeking hack to his utmost speed, which, if not the two-forty quantum, brought them to Sue's much-lauded hotel. There were many such turnouts there; many more arrived afterwards, and Don and Sue being surrounded by birds of their own feather may be considered in their own proper element. Cash and clothing included the two represented probably one hundred dollars, but they confidently believed themselves to be passing off for representatives of one hundred thousand dollars and that made them both feel as if they really did represent that amount. This was immense to some people. "A bird in hand is worth two in a bush" to the Frittakers, to whose fingers nothing will stick. The birds in the bushes are all birds of paradise and the birds in hand peewees and ground chippys, common and easily caught. They have no value in Frittaker eyes, but are contemptible objects of Frittaker scorn.

Neither one of this delectable pair held any or all of the advantages their lives afforded at all comparable with the two or three brief hours of false pretence of that one afternoon. What a pity its golden hours must come to an end! Sweeping of skirts, tossing of heads, contemptuous sniffs and slang phrases, to use a common and expressive one on that occasion, all "dickered out" after supper and strawberries and cream in the dining-room, and bottles, glasses and Havanas in the bar-room. Sue declared it didn't seem like an hour and Don thought it couldn't have been one. And the poor hack—well, no matter what he thought. Don managed to hack him home at a lively rate, where he positively refused to eat oats for two days, no doubt because of his signal failure to palm himself off for the two-forty nag he wasn't, literally was nearly mortified to death. "There's a poisonous drop in the purest cup." If not wholly and solely arsenical, it's wormwoody and gally to that degree you don't care a button which of the three it is. It's enough of either or all of them to embitter one's whole "compos mentis" for the time being. Don felt this intensely on Monday morning. The recollection of Sue's superb airs, the stunning way she queened it among the aristocrats leaving no doubt on their minds that she and Don were creme de la creme, the unexceptional supper, the strawberries and cream of the dining-room, the smashes, juleps and Havanas of the bar-room, all seemed no recompense, after all, for the derisive ha, ha, of the young sport and the mocking he, he, and kiss of his companion. Don was sure they cheapened himself and Sue miserably, and his mind reverted at once to the miserable hack as the sole cause and wished he only had him where he could take satisfaction out of his hide and also the scoundrel who would palm such a brute on a fellow and charge him four dollars, he'd rub him down in a way would do him good. These reflections filled him with fiery indignation and the fiery indignation made him thirsty, so he took another fellow and went to the beer hall and drank beer until his fiery indignation cooled, when Don discovered he had forgotten his pocket-book. Don told the beer man to tick that and it being dinner time he hurried home to get his dinner. After dinner Don looked for his pocket-book and found it under his pillow where he left it. Don thought it sound policy to hold every one for a thief until proven honest, so he proceeded to count his money—one two dollar greenback. Don held it in every position and viewed it in every light and then started to demolish the landlady. He would raze the house to the ground. He'd show her such barefaced robbery wouldn't do. But out in the hall he remembered that he had undertaken a similar feat once before and got razed himself and got into the lockup besides, where, having ample time to count his expenditures as well as his money, was soon convinced that nobody had stolen his money, he not having any left to steal; and now he also remembered that upon that occasion he would have had to go to jail but that his insulted landlady paid his fine, so Don reconsidered his proposed action and fell to counting up costs since Saturday night, which was pay night. Boarding, fourteen dollars; tick at the beer hall, one dollar seventy cents; the cursed old hack, four dollars; toll, seventy-five cents; supper, one dollar and fifty cents; strawberries and cream, fifty cents; smashes, juleps, cigars for himself and five other fellows, two dollars; black-eyed little girl, fifty cents. 'Tis the last feather breaks the camel's back. This last item nearly threw Don into a fit. What kind of a little girl was that? A little girl like that should be rawhided if she ever again presented herself to him. He would never set foot in that door again. Then Don counted up twenty-five dollars from twenty-seven leaves two. Whew! and two weeks to pay night. Would time and space permit a detailed account of Don's financiering from this time forth would edify and instruct the most skillful and expert in the cash department of our "Grindwell governing machine." The masterly lying that tided him out of one straight into and through each succeeding one, not only feeding and clothing himself with the best, but entertaining himself and Sue with drives, picnics, excursions, making the summer for them both one continuous holiday and golden harvest of the fruits of other people's toil, was lying that out-heroded all belief, in fact dimmed the halo around that character in Hudibras who was "for profound and solid lying much renowned," with lying, in short, he paid everything his wages couldn't pay and Don's wages couldn't pay one-half of Don's expenditures. The summer wound up with one of the grandest picnics Don and Sue had ever known, and that picnic, for reasons your veritable historian will now set forth, may be said to be the end of Don's palmy days in our burg.

'Tis a curious fact with regard to the appliances and materials used in clinker factories that they all have a strong tendency to bust; even cold water, a bucketful of which outside of a clinker factory is usually a very harmless agency, inside of one is fearfully destructive unless carefully handled. The day following the great picnic Don's head was full of that jollification. How could he remember the busting propensities and tendencies of things around him? So he gave a bucketful of water a sudden emptying over a mass of molten clinker that busted both water and clinker. The busting scattered it and melted clinker over everybody round, Don excepted, (a fool for luck), but that the blisters of all sizes that operated like the stings of so many hornets gave the recipients of this "fire shower of ruin" enough to do, Don would have had a picnic on hand; would have waltzed him round to the same tune that a picnic that day a year ahead of him eventually did. As it was there was a grand rumpus. The workmen raged, the bosses stormed, most of all the manager (the great "I am" Don called him, swearing that he had his eyes on everything and his nose in everything other people said, that was a manager's business), as if to verify Don's opinion he was instantly on hand and expressed himself so emphatically, though not usually demonstrative, that Don knew but for the great pressure of work and the great scarcity of hands he (Don) would have lit on his head outside the high enclosure. This "jen de esprit" soured the whole establishment, especially the blistered portion of it, who always looked black at Don and hinted broadly at the expediency of hanging a few of the idiots who jeopardize other men's lives with their reckless folly, going themselves scott free of suffering, expense and loss. This was very sour for Don, indeed, so much so that all the balls, oyster suppers, fairs and revivals hardly made amends to Don; in fact, but for Sue 'twould have been insupportable. But suddenly the tension relaxed, another idiot busted another bucket of water and with worse effect, and Don's escapade was forgotten. And this brought the spring and the spring brought the summer and the summer brings picnics. So there was one on the tapis pretty soon. Don, by this time in the matter of tick, was nearly swamped. Creditors' scurvy dogs dogged him everywhere. How to keep enough money out of their clutches to meet the requirements of the picnic was taxing Don's brains to the utmost. Since the calamitous busting of the bucket of water, Don had kept a wary eye on all tools and materials entrusted to his care. The ominous look of the great "I am" on that occasion had made an impression for once on his mental caoutchouc. But his present financial dilemma was enough to obliterate even the existence of the great "I am" in both mind and memory. Lost in abstruse study of the dilemma's manifold horns, a bran-new shovel dropped at Don's heels to lie while he tried to steady his bewildered wits with a glass of beer. But it didn't lie. An ever-watchful, sticky-fingered Frittaker passed that way and the bran-new shovel clave to him. An angry altercation between Don and his boss followed. The ubiquitous "I am" was immediately on hand with a face more ominous than ever. He listened and went away. Saturday was pay night. When Don, in his turn, stood at the window, the cashier, cash in hand, quietly said, "Shovels cost a dollar and half now, Mr. Frittaker." Don felt as if a volcano was lifting him off his feet, but remembering the ominous face of the great "I am," he replied in a tone of cheerful acquiescence that he knew it. The cashier counted out his wages less the price of one shovel and followed up the cash with a brief statement that henceforth the clinker factory would evolute and revolute without Mr. Frittaker's assistance. If Don a minute before felt as if a volcano was lifting him, he now felt as if two volcanoes were lifting him and an earthquake beneath them were urging them to lift. A torrent of abusive billingsgate rushed to his teeth, but somehow circumstances always "cabin crib confine" geniuses of Don's peculiar stamp. A recollection of a former experience rushed with his wrath. On that occasion he had been so indiscreet as to storm the citadel and when, having stormed himself out of breath, he raised the siege he found the tick people bills ready in hand ticking all round him, the news of his dismissal having spread like wildfire. The consequence was they ticked all Don's money out of his hands and when they found it wouldn't go round they threatened to tick his clothes off his back, the hair off his head, the head off his body, and were so manifestly in earnest that Don resolved 'twas the last fandango of that kind should be danced around him. For besides the fright it had cheapened him dismally. His most intimate chums had been lookers-on and had not been slow but rather fast to derisively invite him to go in to walk through the tick people and immediately with surprising impartiality invited and urged the tick people to walk into and go through himself, and when he did escape the contumely of friend and foe, being penniless, was further humiliated by a two-weeks' sojourn in a five-dollar boarding house than which at that time Don knew nothing more thoroughly humbling. So he now clinched his teeth over the lingual lava scorching his tongue, clenched his fist and shook it as near the cashier's nose as he could get it and at his liveliest gait took the directest route to his boarding house and for good or rather bad reasons for the first time entered its rear door. As he entered the voice of Dutch Jake, who was the butt of the Frittaker boarders, resounded through the house. "Yesh, yesh," said Jake, "I bays mine vays. I no sheats nopody." An assertion the landlady in the cheerfulest tone Don had yet heard from her confirmed and applauded. Don applauded, too. "Yes," he muttered, "you cursed idiot." And hurrying to his room hastily bundled up his little all and escaped like a thief in the night the way he entered and without feeling at all cheapened by doing so.

Of the many miseries the poor landlady had to contend with, pay night was the one she dreaded most. Frittakers make one-fourth of the population around a clinker factory, so the landlady invariably had a number of them in her flock, and when they didn't, like Don, sneak off altogether, they invariably endeavored, with excuses more or less paltry or plausible, to escape paying at least a part of their indebtedness. The minute Jake was gone she thought of them and paid a flying visit to their rooms to see who, if any, of them were home, for when they didn't sneak off altogether, if they but escaped her vigilance for but a few hours 'twas almost impossible to collect any part due her before next pay night and the probability was that half and perhaps the whole could never be collected. She came last to Don's room. The door stood open, so did the closet door. The closet will tell she thought, and it did tell that that hopeful cormorant had packed his traps and spread his wings and soared or sailed, 'twasn't a particle of difference which, where it would never pay her to follow, so impenetrable is the network of jurisprudence devised to protect and foster knavery in our free and happy land. The poor woman, at this discovery, looked aghast, then turned and went slowly down stairs repeating drearily enough, "Well, well, well." At the foot of the stairs she turned, hesitated and sighed and called, "Mary,

Mary." "Yes, ma," said a childish voice, and Mary, ready dressed to go out, stood at the head of the stairs. Her mother beckoned, without speaking, and Mary came down. Of late it seemed to the landlady that the poor invalid upstairs could hear every word louder than a whisper spoken in that house, so she whispered, "Mary, dear, I can't let you get your gaiters to-night." A shade of disappointment stole over Mary's childish face, but instantly disappeared and her childish face reflected all the care and anxiety her mother's expressed, when she asked in a tone of alarm: "What has happened, ma?" "Nothing unusual, dear," said her mother, soothingly, "that worthless Don Frittaker has gone without paying me and you know the grocer must be paid to-night and our rent will soon be due." "Yes, ma, I know," said the child, in a tone that at once expressed relief that matters were no worse and commiseration for her poor mother, for whom they were undoubtedly bad enough and would have been made worse by murmuring on her part. "There," continued her mother, "is a dollar. Run for your father's medicine. Don't stay a minute, Mary, dear, you-must see to the supper. I mustn't lose sight of these fellows one minute." And Mary hurried away and her mother's tears started as she thought, "Poor child, poor child, never has an hour to play like any other child; nothing but drudgery, care and anxiety." Two Frittakers entered and her usual struggle with meanness and dishonesty began and taxed her ingenuity and tact to the uttermost. Fifteen boarders who were not Frittakers gave no trouble, payed promptly, spoke kindly and went their way; but these talked interminable lies and larded them with oaths. To these she must plead poverty, must appeal to honesty and honor, where she knew too well there was none; must plead her trying circumstances, her invalid husband, her children, high rent, high markets, high fuel, anything, everything that would touch feeling or touch shame, and all to get money that was justly due her, and all this to night almost failed; would have failed but that the outside pressure made her more determinedly persistent than ever before; and seeing this, they finally with great reluctance and evident indignation, paid the last dollar at last.

So trying was this ordeal that she utterly forgot poor Johnny. He was now her first thought, and one that brought mortal terror. He may be sick unto death, may be dying, may be dead. Frantic at the thought, she sped like an arrow up the stairs and into his room. By the window, in the still moonlight, Johnny sat in his chair bolt upright, so rigid, so death like, her heart stood still and she herself stood as still as her heart. The spectre in the chair drew a long breath, and she sprang to his side. Johnny was fast asleep. Oh, the unexpressible relief. Totally overcome, she sank, rather than crouched, down, on the floor close to his feet, and while he peacefully slept—like Kingsley's poacher's widow—"wept till her heart grew light".

When Don, poised an cormorant wings, took his flight from the landlady's, he directed his course straight to a half-way house he knew of over the river, where he washed, dressed and left his bundle, that he might not

cheapen himself carrying it withal.   Once on the street again, the lingual
lava began anew to scorch his tongue, and his fury at the the great "I am"
anew began to boil over, and whether threats of vengeance or impreca-
tions had the upper hand in his mental retrospection of that gentleman's
merits, t'would be hard to say.   Don vowed, and probably 'twas true, that
of all the "I am's" he had ever known he had always detested this one in
particular, and went on to enumerate various good reasons, among which
there wasn't one of these that follow.   First, the "I am" had started in
life a journeyman clinker-maker, and by his own unaided efforts had risen
to his present position of manager and partner.   This was cheapness Don's
whole soul revolted at.   It meant saving money; it meant steady hard work
day after day, year after year: it meant rigid economy; it meant getting
everything you had honestly—no unpaid tick about it.   All this was most
disgusting to Don, and for the very cheapness of it he hated it.   Indeed, as
Don said to himself with a fearful imprecation, hate was just no name for
what he felt.

When his mental tumult subsided he looked around to see where he
was.   At first that was more than he could divine, but the closed door of a
clinker factory stood just in front of him, and he presently recognized it as an
old acquaintance, and also the fact that he was about three miles from where
he started.   Jing said, "Don, this is just as good a place as I could have
found if I had been looking for one."   To be sure, it was a fellow in those
days could get work anywhere.   All Don needed for the present was a
boarding-house commensurate with his manifold merits.   He soon found one.
It looked for all the world like the one he had left, except the addition of
lace curtains in the parlor windows, and that, in Don' sopinion, was the right kind
of an addition; would be that much added to the halo of importance surround-
ing himself.   Don rang the bell, and when seated in the dining room, stated
his errand.   This brought the landlady, and Don proceeded to inquire
about all the comforts, conveniences and advantages her house afforded.
But she pinned Don suddenly back by stating that her terms were
seven dollars a week in advance, and that he who couldn't pay in advance
(and there was sharpness in her voice) couldn't board with her.
Don's first impulse was to rise and depart, shake the dirt of such presumption promptly from his feet; but then she would have believed that Don was
a fellow without a cent.   He would let her know better, and produced
his pocket book and paid fourteen dollars.   This operated like magic.   The
lady became graciousness itself and conducted Don to the parlor with the lace
curtains, until his supper and room could be prepared for him.   In the parlor with the lace curtains sat a pretty young lady, the landlady's daughter.
Don was duly introduced, and they chatted together, and Don was very
soon convinced that this was a real, true boarding school young lady, quite
different altogether from young ladies who are not boarding school young
ladies; and it struck Don as singular that a fact so striking hadn't struck him
before but that probably arose naturally out of the circumstance that he had

only heard of boarding-school young ladies before, and had seen them merely to the extent of passing them by, which didn't of course, afford the facilities for observation that a stylish parlor with lace curtains did, especially when it contained one of the aforesaid young ladies and himself.

Bye and bye Don was called to supper, and his room not being ready, was again remanded to the parlor. By this time, Don had made up his mind to marry the boarding-school young lady and settle down in life. He had had thoughts of doing so before, but somehow, all the other young ladies he had known, black-eyed Susan included, didn't exactly suit him, undoubtedly because they were not boarding-school young ladies. Don recognized the fact now, that it presented itself to him, and fell to considering how he best could convince the boarding-school young lady that he had graduated from the most of the leading colleges round about. While endeavoring to fix this point and keep conversation afloat, a caller was announced. The boarding-school young lady blushed furiously, and introduced Mr. Sales. Mr. Sales' hair was parted in the middle to that degree that the parting disappeared under his shirt colar and down the middle of his back. His hair was intensely black and crisp, his moustache and teeth were unexceptionable, so was his entire make-up, he being the glass of fashion. Don felt at once that, regarding the matter of graduation, he needn't give himself any further trouble, that this was a dry goods young man, and that his own cake was dough ; and the two volcanos and the earthquake threatened to lift him again, and also urged him to lift the dry goods young man. Happily at this juncture a servant announced that his room was now ready, and he retired without the formality of bidding his new acquaintances good-evening. When a new day dawned on Don (and it was Sunday, too, and of all other days, the one to throw new light), new light dawned upon him regarding boarding-school young ladies. He had always heard they were hum-bugs, and last night's experience confirmed that report certainly, His mind was soon made-up, they should never hum-bug him. But a new girl and a pretty girl he must have, of course. A drive, a ball, a picnic was dullness itself, without a girl, so Don betook himself to church ; knowing full well, that, in every sense, that was the best place to find one. Like gravitates to like. She came into the pew and sat down beside him. Another Susan Frittaker with this sligth distinctive difference : her eyes were blue, she was very pretty, her dress had the very latest extreme touches of fashion on and about it. Yet, not withstanding, Don took the wise precaution of convincing himself, by observation, that there was none other there that excelled her, before he gave himself away. Which, when he sat about it, he did with zeal and fervor, and he soon saw indications that Sue number two would probably accept the gift. He managed in a few days to procure an introduction, and Don was fairly settled for awhile at least, and the old routine of picnics, excursions, and tick began anew, and went on swimmingly, until near the close of summer. While Don was thus roping himself, and Sue number two in that Sunday evening, Sue number one was wondering what in the world had become of him, not having heard of his dismissal, and the black-eyed little girl, fermented with impatience, and finding that didn't produce Dan, tell to fermenting the rest of the family, by a pertinacious effort to send them in all directions to look for Don ; and persisted until each in turn had boxed her ears, Sue boxing them twice to make sure she hadn't omitted to box them once. This convinced the black-eyed little girl that her ears would do for to-night, so she went to bed, the others soon following : Sue beginning to wonder if it could be possible Don was looking for another girl to take to the picnic and mentally vowing vengeance, if such should be so.

Next morning, while Sue was tidying the parlor, a gossipy Frittaker passing with a bucket of water, looked in, and seeing Sue, set her bucket down, fixed a scrutinizing gaze on Sue's face and asked, "What was Don Frittaker dismissed for?" Whatever Sue's feelings might be, she wasn't the girl to show them indiscreetly, so she said with a nonchalant air that looked as if she might feel interested, that she wondered why Don wasn't round yesterday. The gossipy Frittaker had calculated on something else than this, for it nonplussed, wholly disconcerted her. She dropped the subject, lifted the bucket and said she must hurry home, and Sue shut the door. When she turned round the black-eyed little girl stood like a statue just behind her. The black-eyed little girl's mouth and eyes had a fixed expression as if they had suddenly petrified, and now she as suddenly doubled from her waist down, "whoo whoo oo-oo-oo!" she roared. This was so unexpected it took Sue's breath away, and set her mother, who was sewing at the window, bolt upright in her chair. Whaa-whaa wa-wa wa haa'd" the little girl.

"What on earth do you mean?" exclaimed Sue, recovering her breath. " Wou, wou, oo, oo, oo!" howled the little girl, again doubling up. "What do you mean?" screamed Sue, seizing the plait of hair that hung down the little girl's back with one hand, and the fire shovel with the other. "Yow-yow-yow-yow-yow-yow!" yowed the little girl, but she didn't double up this time. Sue held the plait too tight. Sue plied the shovel round the little girl's shoulders, asking with every flap what she meant. Their mother, joining in, tried to grasp the shovel with one hand and the little girl's arm with the other, and getting hold of it shook furiously. "Whaa-mu-r-r-r-der-mur-r-r-der!" shrieked the little girl. "Hush, hush," cried Sue and her mother both in a breath. "Shut up, shut up in one minute; shut up; what's the matter with you? I'll send to the mill for your father," said their mother. "My, my, my!" sobbed the little girl, "that st-stinkin' Don Frittaker's gone n-n-n I ain't go-got but ni-nine dollars that wo-won't buy me n-no-silk dress so it wo-won't" "You a silk dress!" exclaimed Sue. "I'd talk about it. I must have five dollars of that money to help buy my lace sacque. I haven't enough." "Whoo-whoo ow-mu-r-r-der!" roared the little girl, and now she assumed the offensive and attacked Sue with her teeth and nails. "Ye shan't, ye shan't!" she shrieked, and their mother stamped on the floor, shook the little girl, and Sue again pulled the plait and flapped her shoulders with the shovel.

But here the echo of voices and heavy feet came in from the side alley, the tumult instantly ceased. "Oh!" said Sue, in a terrified whisper, "there's pap and Bob and there ain't a drop of coffee!" Oh, then there was marshalling in hot haste; all three made a rush for the back stair, but their mother had the fore way and escaped, leaving poor Sue to face the music, which she did by seizing the coffee mill, and the way that coffee mill went round was a caution to all the coffee mills ever was made, and the way pap and Bob swore when they discovered the situation beat all the swearing you ever heard; it made poor Sue's black eyes look blue, and she was used to it. Pap and Bob both looked as if they meditated a rush for her black hair, but at that moment pap's eyes fell on the tearful face of the black-eyed little girl. "What ails you," he thundered, and instantly his heavy hand on the side of her head made her reel and shriek and fly up stairs. "Here, you," shouted the savage creature, "stop there." The little girl, half way up, stopped instantly. "Now, shut right up," thundered the brute, and she did, there wasn't another word.

By this time Sue had jingled the necessary dishes, bread, butter, meat and coffee, on the table. Pap and Bob each snatched a chair and set it down with a twist as if it had been a wrench, and fell to pouring boiling coffee down their throats mumbling, with their mouths stuffed full, that it wasn't fit to drink. Sue produced a jelly cake that had been kept over for Don Frittaker, and the two semi-savages dropped the bread and butter they were devouring and fell voraciously upon it, their tempers and tones mellowing at once. Sue followed it up with a pie and the mumbling growl died away like the mutterings of distant thunder after a summer storm. When they had eaten and drank everything on the table they left, and when the sound of their feet told they were out of hearing Sue said solemnly, "Well, you're a pair of hogs, that's what you are." And now, having time to spare, she proceeded to pay her compliments to Don Frittaker. "Well, I do declare," she said, "that nasty, dirty, stinking Don Frittaker's gone, and the picnic comes off Thursday, only to think, I sacked Joe for that slink, and now Joe's married." And Joe being married, led to other reflections of the same general tenor.

In the afternoon she made calls, one of them at Vivian Frittaker's boarding house. Vivian was at home. The picnic was the absorbing topic, of course, and among other arrangements made for it, Vivian arranged to escort Sue, and calling in the following evening to talk the matter over, the little black-eyed girl sat down beside him and told him how Don had always given her a quarter when he came; so Vivian gave her one, too, and the black-eyed little girl went into the usual ecstacy of gratitude and delight, and slid off her chair and departed, saying to herself, "Ah, ha, Lizzy Frittaker, see if I don't have a silk dress and a better one than yours!" and

Sue pronounced Vivian a far nicer fellow than Don—so genteel—and from that day to this nobody in that house, not even the black-eyed little girl, ever thought of Don Frittaker again, and truth to tell, Don Frittaker thought just as little about them, although the only perceptible difference between his new Susan and his old one was in the color of their eyes. Don was delighted with it, and being happily clear of all the old tick and in a locality that offered fair opportunity for accumulating new tick, he turned his wages to the very best account in the matter of amusement for the delectation of his new Susan and himself, and accomplished this so well that he hardly knew where he was till the summer was over; in fact, was being closed by one last grand picnic, and Don and his blue-eyed Susan were closing it splendidly in a cotillion set, balance all-hands round. "Don, Don," said a fellow standing behind Don when Don and his partner came to a standstill after promenade all. " What is this Jay Cooke business anyhow!" "Jay Cooke, Jay Cooke," said Don. "Hanged if I know; what was he, what did he do?" "Oh," said another fellow, "busted up, that's all." "Oh, Oh!" said Don, "kind of cooked Jay!" "He! he! he!" tittered Susan. "Well, did I ever! ha! ha! ha!" Encouraged by this, Don grew witty, and asked if he was a blue Jay, or if anybody had ever heard of a black Jay, and threw Sue into convulsions of laughter, that was suddenly terminated by her brother and three other fellows who had danced and drank themselves into a very inflammatory state of mind, and now, in consequence, wound up the set they were dancing by setting their teeth, and setting to work with their eight clenched fists to demolish one another. And one being Susan's brother, Don fell to expostulating, hoping to make peace, but the moment Don turned in as a peace-maker the entire quartette turned in to make pieces of Don and would assuredly have made a thousand pieces of him in an incredibly short time had not every fellow that could get a hand in stuck that hand in up to his elbow and grasped wherever he could take hold. They who caught the quartette thrapples, choking with all their might and they who caught the quartette's hair or heels, pulling with all their might, finally dragging them off.

Don dropped out of their clutches helpless, senseless as a sack of oats (wild oats probably), falling on his face. A half dozen fellows laid hold of him and turned him over; one whistled a prolonged "Whew!" one laconically remarked that "that was a settler," to which all the lookers-on assented. Don neither assented nor dissented; was mute as a mouse. If he had had ever so much to say he had no mouth to say it with, that organ and every other feature of his face having disappeared, leaving a puffy mass that strikingly resembled a conglomerate of sausage meat and cinders. "Oh, good heaven!" said blue-eyed Susan to Ad. Frittaker, "isn't that awful! he's killed ain't he?" "Most like," said Ad., "if he ain't he ought to be, the darned fool." "Come, there's the band; hurry, hurry, we'll miss this set." "Oh," said Sue, "Indeed I—" "Hurry, hurry," said Ad, seizing her arm, and Sue hurried, and, having her reputation of being a first-class dancer to sustain, had no time to think of Don again until the picnic was over, and when the picnic was over nobody knew where Don was taken to, and everybody said he would die anyhow, so there was no use thinking about him. And Sue never thought any more about him.

Meanwhile the four piece-making worthies were dragged to a quiet nook where a thorough examination, to ascertain what damage they had received and what the quarrel was about, lasted so long they all four were so drunk as to be incapable of doing further mischief that day. So one that was able to sit up was propped against the trunk of a tree, and the three who were unable to sit up were carefully laid backwards across a dry, sunny log, so they wouldn't smother for one thing, and so they would be safe where they could be found again, for another. To this log Don was carried until something or other, nobody knew what, could be done for him. One suggested that he should be taken home, so another was dispatched to ascertain where Don lived, but he fell to dancing and forgot about it. Another was dispatched to see what fellow number one was doing, but he fell to drinking and forgot about it, and presently they were all gone wherever their half-drunken fancies led them. All but the driver of a wagon that brought forage to the picnic, who finding no one left but himself to do anything, set about doing something in good earnest. With the greatest difficulty he succeeded in getting three or four half-drunken loons to assist him put the speechless, senseless, helpless Don into the wagon, which done, not all the blustering he could bring to bear on anybody and everybody could produce the information where Don should be taken to. Finally being left all to himself and being a sticky fingered Frittaker and in close proximity to the dry, sunny log, it struck him very forcibly that the pockets of the three safe ones across the log would probably throw light on the subject, he lost not a minute in going through them, and the collective pockets of the safe ones threw light to the amount of about three dollars in fractional currency, which enabled him to see his way so clearly that he transferred the currency to his own pocket, transferred himself to the seat of his wagon and put spurs to his steed with the lash of his whip and rattled off with Don at such a lively gait that Don's teeth, that had all been in his jaws in the morning but were now all in the pit of his stomach, danced quite as lively as Sue at that minute was dancing with Ad Frittaker. Guided by the light of the fractional currency, the driver found Don's landlady's door as if by instinct. The door stood open, and the driver took Don by the collar and shouldered him like the beforementioned sack of oats, toted him into the hall, where he dumped him in a grey sodden heap on the floor, kicked the door until the house shook, sprang into his wagon and turned the very first corner he came to.

The alarm brought the landlady up from the basement, who, when her eyes fell upon the grey heap, eyed it a little and said, "Oh, whiskey, whiskey." Then after a pause, added, "Which of them is it I wonder," and going round the grey heap to see, recognized Don's new suit and said, "Why, it's Don, and Oh, goodness, his face is one complete smash!" She listened a minute to his heavy breathing. "Aye, aye, the game's up with you," she added, and turning hastily, ran upstairs to Don's room, and to the closet of it which she opened, and at once proceeded to take an inventory of its contents, which resulted in one pair of dirty pants, with strong indication of open-rupture at the knees before very long, one awful dirty and very thin flannel shirt, one dirty muslin shirt that was of no account, one clean muslin shirt gone all to the bad, another clean shirt going all to the bad as fast as it could, one dickey all fringy 'round the collar and breast, another dickey that was simply a breastwork of strings, one pocket handkerchief full of holes, another that wasn't full of holes (this was a lady's and had her initials in one corner, and the landlady, being a sticky-fingered Frittaker, jumped at the conclusion that Don's fingers had stuck to something at last, and as it wasn't his, stuck it into her own pocket), an old pair of socks without toes or heels, another pair that were legs only, a worn-out tooth brush, a coarse comb with five teeth, a fine comb without any teeth, three cigar stumps; a bit of tobacco, two pieces of a cork-screw, one Jew's harp and two cards, the last of a pack, one the ace of spades, the other the king of trumps. The ace of spades might have been the ace of shovels for anything the landlady knew or cared, but the king of trumps she lifted and viewed thoughtfully, and said softly, "Oh, Don, my boy, you were the king of trumps yourself." Little she dreamed that Don might eventually prove the king of tramps, for at that minute she believed the last trump to be trumping loud as it could toot in Don's ears in the hall below.

And full of this belief, she lifted a castor oil bottle that towered, head and shoulders, above half a dozen empty cologne and bear's oil bottles, turned it sideways, eyed the spoonful or so of oil it contained, and said, "Yes, yes, and you've got your last physic, Don," and with that she took out all the articles of clothing, the handkerchief full of holes included, glanced at a heap of valentines, photographs and love letters that would have filled a peck, slipped her disengaged hand under and up through them as if to convince herself: her eyes did not deceive her, sniffed contemptuously, and ejaculating, "The ass, the ass!" closed the door with a bang. Than which action it seems to your historian, nothing could more sufficiently prove the efficiency of a boarding-school education and the sound philosophy of parting one's hair down the middle of one's back, for although the ignorant unphilosophic landlady dismissed a peck of love letters, valentines and photographs with one contemptuous sniff, her boarding-school daughter and the dry goods young man could by no means express all their views and opinions with regard to them in the three hours they that evening devoted to the important subject, and were obliged to adjourn that meeting to one at the earliest possible date for a further consideration of it.

The landlady's two sons were running night turn in a clinker factory hard by. She now gave them a day turn that turned them both out of bed and dressed them to boot in about two jiffies. When they reached the hall below a bundle lay on one side of Don, and his working clothes on the other, and the boys having had a day turn themselves, now proceeded to give Don one that turned him out of his best clothes into his worst ones with a celerity that, so far as known, greatly exceeded Don's own best efforts. This done, the boys turned back the way they came, and turned into bed again, their mother presently following with Don's new suit, which she put carefully away, but not with the love letters, castor oil and Jew's harp. This done, she put on her shawl and bonnet and went—well, no matter where she went; she'll be back pretty soon.

When three or four women *foregather on a sidewalk, three or four more will presently join them, and of all the vehicles in the world no vehicle in the world will foregather women like a peddler's wagon. When the landlady returned pretty soon, 'twas with a potato peddler and his wagon. The wagon was empty. Three or four women, the landlady's nearest neighbors, foregathered at once and the landlady explained the situation. By this time the three or four other women had put in their appearance and the landlady explained the situation again. Thereupon all the foregathered women overflowed with sympathy, mostly for Don at the first, mostly for the landlady at the last. "Come, come, me wumman, what did ye breng me here fur?" asked the potato peddler, who was an Irishman. This brought the landlady to the exigencies of the case which she at once explained to the foregathered women by stating that when the beds in a boarding-house are made up in the morning they are made up for all day, and can by no possibility be unmade that day again; that to let Don, in his present condition ride in a wagon without a bed in it would be inhuman cruelty on the part of the foregathered women, who were, of course, charitable, and one of them especially pious, to whom she broadly intimated that the piety that couldn't stand the lending of a bed was piety that was of no account. This was efficacious for the pious woman turned into her house and presently turned out again with a bed and a face that somehow looked longer than when she turned in, no doubt from excess of pious enthusiasm, "Mrs. G," said the landlady, "havn't you got a pillow?" What woman hasn't a number of pillows? How could she pretend to say she hadn't one? So she didn't bandy words, but went and brought one and was done with it (in more senses than one). "Now," said the landlady, "if we only had Don in the wagon. I expect (looking around), 'twill keep us all pretty busy to put him in." Then headed by the Irish potato man, they proceded to the hall, where the Irish potato man took charge of Don's head, as he sagely remarked, to see and keep the strain off it, and the landlady took charge of Don's feet to see and keep the strain off them. And then, with that wonderful readiness of faculty characteristic of superior executive ability, the landlady and the Irish potato man ranged the foregathered women equally on each

* Scotch—To meet accidently.

man solemnly adjuring them to "tak' a guid grupp and howld for their very dear lives," (and one of the women expressing some doubts on the subject), himself and the landlady both in a breath assured them they could with perfect safety strain any amount so they only lifted enough.

These preliminaries settled, the cavalcade started and the foregathered woman lifted nobly, the Irish potato man assured them that of it, by a constant repetition of bully, bully, which brought them in good time and good order to the side of the wagon. "Now then, up, up ! heave yo all hands," said the Irish potato man, and the foregathered women heaved, and Don balanced most equitably for a moment on the edge of the wagon box, and then suddenly dropped in a very cheap sort of a way, indeed, to the bottom of it. "Hould hard there, me boy," said the Irish potato man, in a loud tone of stern authority, that struck mortal terror to the heart of the foregathered women. What had they done ? Was he killed ? would they all get hanged for it ? and they each and all opened their mouths and gazed with horror at one another with them. But as not one of them knew better than another, whether they could, would, or should be hanged, or not, they all turned to the Irish potato man, who had mounted his wagon and to their great relief, he only said: "Come now, skip up here some o' ye and help me *whammel him in the bed." But a look of fixed determination came over every face of the foregathered women. A risk like that, (whatever it had been,) they could not, would not run again. The landlady, seeing this, skipped herself and skipped like a lamplighter, too, and the potato man and she whammeled Don and she skipped out again, alightening on the ground, with the bound of an india rubber ball. "Now," she exclaimed triumphantly, "if we only had a comfort to cover him, he's all ready." Again the foregathered women opened their mouths and looked at one another with them this time, with an expression as if each was going to ask the other where all this was going to end. The land lady understood it and added deprecatingly, addressing one in particular, that any old thing would do. "Come ! come !" said the Irish potato man, "I can't stand here all day, and the fellow needs a comfort, and a good, warm one, too." To be sure, he did ; although 'twas late October, 'twas warm as July ; and this showed that the Irish potato man knew what he was talking about, and the sequel showed that he had a keen eye to business, when he said it, and his saying it when he did, brought the foregathered woman in particular right up to the scratch at once ; for she shut her mouth as if she were shutting it for good and all, and went and brought a comfort such as he prescribed.

The landlady put a greenback in his hand and said, "To the West Penn," but whether that were a pig pen or not, the Irish potato man didn't ask, but put the greenback in his pocket, winked with a look of profound sagacity at the landlady, bowed with a convulsive expression of countenance

---

*Scotch.— Turned him around.

side of the solidly substantial portion of Don's *habeas corpus*, the Irish potato to the foregathered women and said, "Oh! ye're beauties ivery wan av ye," whereat the foregathered women again opened their mouths and looked, every one at the other, to see if she believed it or not, and seeing plainly that the other hadn't the least doubt of it, she believed it, too, and it being a highly satisfactory article of faith, they unanimuosly smiled their approbation and disforegathered each to her separate home. And the Irish potato man peddled away with Don, and actually peddled him to the West Penn, (which proved to be a hospital,) instead of into the river, but never, no never peddled bedding or potatoes up that street or down that street that passes the landlady's door.

"Well!" said the surgeon of the West Penn to his assistant, thrusting his hands deep into his pockets, while taking in the situation as presented by the conglomerate of sausage meat and cinders, "Well, that was a glorious jamboree and a high old time." He was right, and he might have added that Don's whole life had been jamboree, more or less, and that Don had managed to infuse more or less jamboree into the lives of all he came in contact with. But this surgeon was no moralizer nor metaphysical speculator, but a German of the most practical stamp, and devoted himself to surgery of the most practical stamp, as we shall see. For he immediately took the case of instruments the assistant held, selected a handful of glittering hooks and prongs, and began to plow deep in the sausage meat and cinders. Presently a hook stuck fast somewhere, the surgeon gave a hefty tug, and the end of Don's nose came to the surface. This was encouraging and encouraged by it, the surgeon, with renewed ardor, resumed the plowing. Presently an eye made its appearance; this, the surgeon manipulated tenderly and dexterously, and finally landed it safely in its proper socket, the other was soon fished up and landed too, and the surgeon, by extreme care and good management, succeeded in properly adjusting them both. "Charming," said the surgeon to his assistant, the periphery of whose eyes and circumference of whose mouth had perceptibly widened as the operation progressed. "Charming! they're both as good as new," if I can only discover the whereabouts of his mouth, I'll soon have him all right again. If any doubt of this lurked in the assistant's mind, he gave it no expression, from which I conclude there was no doubt of it lurking in his mind, nor can I see how a doubt of it could lurk in anybody's mind. Whether or not, the surgeon plowed deeper than ever, saying as he did so, that if a fellow had an opening anywhere in his face that would lead to his stomach, he could get along. Upon hearing this new and valuable surgical axiom, the assistant immediately drew out his note book, and made a note of it—which was quite correct; axioms should never be permitted to go to loss, especially surgical axioms, and if by any possibility, the eyes and mouth of the surgeon's assistant could have widened any more, your historian has no doubt they would have widened when an axiom like this was announced.

Deftly, the surgeon plied the handful of hooks and prongs, and the sausage meat and cinders underwent that curious transformation, that froth undergoes when you stir it about—disappears under your eyes, but how, or when, or where, you never can tell—anyhow its gone. The outline of an opening grew distinctly visible ; the surgeon gave a screw and a sudden twist at one side, as if he was anchoring something, and dropped the handful of instruments, exclaiming triumphantly, "Now then, ain't I hard to beat ?" the assistant triumphantly assented by trying to close his mouth and eyes again, and was rather more surprised than delighted, to find that he couldn't. But your historian, who can open and shut hers at pleasure, does declare and affirm, and will maintain it in the face of all opposition, that this is a surgeon and-a half and a surgeon that can't be beat, let the other come from where he may. And don't it beat the very deuce anyhow, that one on all occasions must buckle on their armor and grind their battle axe and put on war paint, and breathing threatening and slaughter, rush to the front in defense of incomparable ability, as I do now in defense of this surgeon, who, in the very nature of things, should need no defending ; his manifold merits, and their incalcuable value being self evident. Yet, if I didn't as I do, with war paint and tomahawk, intimidate the constitutional grumblers, they would be forever in the front, storming like mad.

What business had he with Don Frittaker, they would all howl together. Who wanted the worthless brute to live? Of what good is he, the abominable, contemptible, lying, cheating villain? Who thanks the old Dutch butcher knife for grubbing around in the disgusting rotten smear and fishing out his brazen snoot and patching it up? The welfare of the public, they storm, should be the first consideration of every surgeon and every historian. How is the welfare of the public conserved by remodelling this degraded brute, who, as long as there is a breath in him, will only grow in brutality. And then everybody is madder than ever, and set about investigating and pitch into your historian. We don't believe, say they, that this alleged history is history at all. A surgeon like that is a fool, and a historian like this is an idiot. If your alleged history is anything but lies, Don Frittaker had no business there. Nobody had any business to send him there. It's very well understood, they growl, that we never gave our hard-earned money to prolong the existence of vicious criminals; that we built and we support the institution for worthy unfortunates. And this brings the officials in a body to the front. And they swell the clamor with their protestations. Nobody wanted him here; his being here was all a mistake, somebody blundered. This institution is not for such trash, is not free to any body but officials, and their families. Other people pay, of course.

Worse and worse, the grumblers all howl together. Everybody has to pay in this free institution but you and your families, you and your families use up all the State appropriations appropriated out of our pockets, and all private bequests and we in our misfortune get in to pay and pay roundly. Whew! this is news; a fine kettle of fish; and Dutch surgeon; and drivelling idiot that writes his history. So now you see clearly why I always wear war paint and a sharp tomahawk and stand in the front. Nothing meritorious could stand on the face of the earth if I didn't.

"Now then," said the surgeon when their little jubilation was over, "now then, the needle and plaster." Both were immediately forthcoming, and the surgeon stitched here and stitched there, and the assistant plastered plaster everywhere, until Don's physiognomy disappeared under it altogether. When both surgeon and assistant exclaimed "Well done," and the surgeon added, "Now, my boy, in three weeks you'll have a new face, good bye." Don, thankless creature, said nothing not even good bye. But when three weeks after he stood ready to depart on the threshold of the West Penn, he had a new face. So completely and thoroughly new it was that nobody could or would have suspected that he was the real original Don Frittaker. And as it devolves upon your historian to give a full and reliable "diagnostrum of its newness" your historian unhesitatingly pronounces Don's new mouth the newest part of his new face. It would undoubtly have been perfectly circular but for one of those peculiar whorls characteristic of some univalve shells, this whorl was at the side where the surgeon gave the finishing twist and anchored something, and gave the beholder an ineradicable impression that Don's new mouth would henceforth, like a pitcher, empty at one side on the circular side of Don's mouth, its new lips were strangely rigid as if they might be lined with tin—copper-bottomed with it, as a sailor would say. His new nose unpleasantly suggested a half-way measure that the surgeon had adopted to get an unpleasant and troublesome piece of business off hand; his new eyes, each in its way painfully endeavoring to get a look behind Don's back, which, if they succeeded in doing, would certainly have been very useful and advantageous to Don. And now your historian assures everybody that this is a full and in every particular reliable diagnostrum, and no mistake. As I said before and repeat now, your historian could not by any possibility make a mistake.

Yes, Don Frittaker stands on the threshold of the West Penn hospital ready to embark again on the river of life; but, alack-a-day I'm sorry to say, that barrin' the matter of the new face, Don in all other respects was the old Don, for a nurse who had been particularly kind and attentive to him, had besides lent him a dollar, he forgot to bid good bye with, while another fellow who one day threatened to put a new head on Don (as if the new one he had wasn't new enough) he hardly could part with, so affected was he that his new eyes overflowed with tears and his new mouth threatened to do the same at the emptying side.

Of all the occurrences since the picnic Don remembered nothing. The picnic and his life previous to it he remembered very well, and one of the things he remembered best was the new suit of clothes he wore on that occasion, and as he had regularly paid his landlady in advance, for the good reason she wouldn't be paid any other way, he could with perfect safety claim them, and not doubting that that worthy lady had them he went directly back from the West Penn to her house. When he announced himself as being Don Frittaker, to say the landlady was amazed is to put the case very mildly, and that for reasons of her own she was very unwilling to believe it and positively refused to do so at first, is not at all surprising, but Don persisting in insisting that he was himself and furthermore describing and demanding his new suit, she reluctantly, improbable as it appeared, admitted that he might be himself, but that she might have his new suit she pronounced an utter impossibility, and to prove it, she related with many embellishments, the charitable liberality of herself and neighbors in providing bedding and conveyance at their own expense and seeing that Don was still incredulous (and when Don's new face expressed incredulity it was wonderful to look upon), she took him out with her and loudly summoned the foregathered women to corroborate her testimony with their own, intimating with considerable feeling that an unjust and injurious accusation was made against her impliedly, if not openly, and that their sympathies were now requisite and confidently expected. But the foregathered women, whose bedding had floated away on the last tide of sympathy, couldn't be induced to foregather on the sidewalk this time. They contented themselves with taking in the situation from their upper windows where, when convinced that their wordly goods were perfectly safe, they one and all vehemently asseverated the landlady's innocence and as vehemently asseverated the Irish potato man's guilt, assuring Don that an Irish potato man who would steal bedding would steal the very best clothing in the world, and had assuredly stolen his. Nevertheless the contortions of incredulity in Don's new countenance only contorted the more, and the landlady seeing this, took effective measures to get quit of Don by fixing her eyes intently on the whorl at one side of Don's new mouth. It is indeed, very singular that this mouth that was the surgeons *Chef de œuvre*, the acme, as it were, of his achievements in the matter of mouth-making, and consequently his pride and glory, was held by Don in great abomination, he could neither bear to look at it himself nor endure any other body to do so. Our wide-awake landlady perceived this, and turned it to her own account, and by so doing soon disconcerted Don, and to that extent that his memory was refreshed and he recollected that he had never paid one dollar on his suit, that in fact it didn't belong to him and couldn't therefore be any loss to his own pocket, and a conviction seizing him that the landlady was scrutinizing his detestable mouth that she might be able to report it fully to her boarding school daughter and the dry goods young man, he made his escape at once and went at once in search of a new boarding house and being financially bankrupt was fain to seek refuge in a five dollar one. When it rains calamity it always pours; besides, the standing aggravation of this mouth he never bargained for, and the mortification of a cheap boarding house on a back street new difficulties presented themselves. Don soon found that that Jay Cooke business was going to cook himself, do him brown in fact; many of the clinker factories that before it were running double turn, didn't turn at all now; others that were turning single turn, the great "I am's" said were turning oftener than circumstances warranted. It was not now great pressure of work and scarcity of hands but great pressure of hands and scarcity of work, and the great "I am's" were sagely turning this to their own advantage. For years they had been robbed by the thriftless unprincipled, unscrupulous Don Frittakers, who never do a fair days work for their day's wages if they can help it; who never care a button for their employers property or interests, who if they could safely destroy either would rather do so, than not; who never care a button for the safety of other peoples' limbs, or lives; never a button for the misery, suffering, and loss their misconduct and recklessness entail upon their fellow beings. The "I am's" had endured and tolerated the nuisance just as other nuisances often must be and are tolerated until opportunity offers for abating them.

Now they were abating the Frittaker nuisance. Honorable, honest workmen could now be had in abundance and no Frittaker could get work, neither could our Don, from any employer who had ever employed him before; result—he must tramp, steal or starve. Don tramped. And for tramping he was fully prepared—no money, no clothes, no reputation for anything good. A tramp's complete outfit and the winter just setting in, nothing could be more propitious. Don set out. Good-bye, Don. This world of ours is one of the very few things that can turn and turn and still go on. This world of ours has turned and gone on precisely the same as before ever since Don left us three years ago. Whether Don turned and turned while he went on your historian don't know nor does she know whether it was the world's turning or Don's own turning brought Don back to Pittsburg, anyhow Don is back. Don set the fact forth very lugubriously in a letter to an evening paper some four or five weeks ago. I've got another day turn, says Don. A conscienceless landlord gives it to me, says Don. Its diluted water, mackerel bones and beans some other fellow didn't leave, says Don. Its peppered with dirt, says Don, and salted with filth, says Don, and it's fifteen cents a jarum, says Don, and this last feather breaks the back of Don's temper, as whilom did the black-eyed little girl business, and Don waxeth exceeding wrathy and quotes Shakespeare. Oh, shade of Dogberry, Don Frittaker quote Shakespeare! How that stirs the innermost soul of your historian. Did you when in the flesh ever outsport discretion in this sort, Dogberry? What! Who is that says I *must* be mistaken? That, this *can't* be Don Frittaker? That Don Frittaker couldn't spout Shakespeare if he'd try. Haven't I told you over and over, I don't make mistakes. But you shall see. I'll ask. For one must show some people proof of everything. Did he come to your office, Mr. Editor? did you see him? had he a new mouth? did his mouth empty at one side? Was his new nose an abridged Missouri compromise? Were both his new eyes trying to get a peep at the rear of his back? But what's the use of asking? Don't I know there can be no mistake? Who but Don would while away his time spooning at a dirt-begrimed shadow of nothing? Who but he would hold it between him and the sky with a fork for a better contemplation of its true inwardness? Who but he would pay fifteen cents more than once for such a culinary hallucination when in any grocery he could buy a loaf of excellent bread for six cents a pound, of excellent crackers for six and a quarter, pound of first-class cheese, dry beef, bologna or a quarter peck of apples for 5 cents? No brain but a brain like his could touch such an imbecile depth of inanity? None other than he could tramp past a thousand opportunities of doing better with his last fifteen cents, and never think or say, I can and I will do better. Yes, your historian knows this is one or the other of the pick and choice of Dons you can have by calling at the conscienceless landlord's institution. His report for January is in her hand, which states that one thousand and fifty-nine Don Frittakers were admitted there during that month, of these nine hundred and six were unmarried men and widowers. Of the entire number admitted one thousand and twenty-one were in good health; plenty of Dons certainly. But the Don who grappled so valiantly with the dirt begrimed shadow was not the only Don of them who "outsported discretion" in the columns of the papers.

Another yowls a terrible yowl and asserts that two-thirds of the great army of tramps were made such under a Republican administration, and are not tramps of choice, but necessity. What a horrible thing a Republican administration is! And what a strange thing it is that ALL the men under it don't tramp! How do so many manage to stay at home? How do they manage to get homes (and homes of their own, too) to stay in? Suppose your historian would show Don how some things can be done just as well as others under a Republican administration. Here is my excellent neighbor, Mr. K. Six years ago he came to work in the clinker-factory, bringing his wife and two children. They rented a house of one very large room on a lot eighteen by ninety feet. This couple are Germans in Germany, well-to-do people, breakfast on bread and coffee; dinner consists of bread, potatoes, kraut, bacon or pork; in the country, milk; in the towns, beer; supper, bread and coffee. As a rule, well-to-do people in Germany live all their lives, Sundays and holidays excepted, on this fare, and are strong, healthy and happy as the average American. Mr. K and his excellent wife having lived so in Germany, and seeing that by living so in these United States they could, although Mr. K was only a laborer, save money and buy property, they, without any philosophizing, set about it. To-day he owns the little house, has built a kitchen back of it, a cellar under it, has paid for it and also bought and partly paid for another lot, and has meanwhile fed and clothed himself, wife and children. They have five now, and no man can say that this excellent citizen ever cheated him out of a dollar. I select him and the others I shall mention because I personally know and can vouch for their honesty.

Another who came about the same time to seek his fortune in our burg and went to work in our clinker factory, rented one of the same row of little houses, had a wife and five children. They too lived on the same fare, they, too, were Germans; he, too, was a laborer in the clinker factory. His good wife is a marvel of enterprise and industry. She kept cows, took washing, sold yeast, goes out nursing the sick, and I look as I write this, on their new house, cellar, hall, four large rooms, finished garret, built in excellent style on two large lots on a first-class street, costing in all not less than three thousand dollars, and, I'm told, paid for, as has meanwhile been every article of food, clothing or other necessaries of life they ever used. They also own and have paid for two of the litttle houses they formerly lived in. Another who started at the same time, in the same row of houses and under similar circumstances, owns two of the houses and a dairy of fourteen cows. That marvelous model of sticky fingered Frittaker ingenuity, the Universal Trust Company gobbled up two hundred and fifty of this worthy couple's hard-earned dollars. In the same row of little houses, some five years ago, came a little Dutch woman who should put to shame every beggar and tramp in these United States. Her husband is dead; she is childless, friendless; she has supported herself through long years by gathering, drying and selling herbs—not a profitable business by any means; she attends market in all weather, is nearly seventy-five years of age, has bought and paid for her little house within the last five years.

And into the head-quarters of the mackerel bones there tramped last month, 6 bakers, 12 bricklayers, 10 boiler-makers, 8 butchers, 9 clerks, 20 carpenters, 10 cooks, 7 cigar-makers, 29 farmers, 35 moulders, 31 miners, 24 machinists, 31 painters, 18 printers, 11 puddlers, 12 railroaders, 17 sailors, 16 shoe-makers, 13 stone cutters, 5 tinners, 5 tailors, 6 weavers, 698 laborers, of whom 972 were unencumbered by families, and who for the seven or eight years preceding the last three years must have earned wages varying from two to five dollars per day, according to their occupation. Oh, whiskey, whiskey! Oh, imbecile depths of inanity: But what's the use of preaching:

Almost every phase of domestic life is represented on our burg. One and all of its well-to-do inhabitants have had more or less of the difficulties and obstacles that impede human progress to contend with, one and all, without exception, have had to contend with these disadvantages wherewith a Republican administration floored this one thousand and fifty Don Frittakers, yet they are not floored. On the contrary, they flourish simply by having practiced such wise precepts as "a penny saved is a penny earned," "take care of the pennies, and the pounds will take care of themselves," when wages were good and work abundant. If Don instead of spitting tobacco juice over the enterprising people vastly superior to him and fumbling in a dazed way through Charles Reade's "Put Yourself in His Place," would open his eyes to what men who have families to support can and do accomplish, would see how well they support their families while acquiring property, and a good deal of it, Don might be a wiser, if not a better man. Our burg is a quite a town, and with the exception of the clinker factory, and some forty or fifty dwellings belonging to it, has been built within the last seven years by mechanics and laborers who supported families ranging from three to seven members; men whose wives, though just as willing to assist their husbands, as the wives I have mentioned, were wholly unable to do so otherwise than by prudent management of their households. And Don might also learn another important fact, that those men would one and all be better off to-day but for the various ways in which they have been robbed by the comtemptible, despicable Frittakers, sticky and slippery fingered both—the Frittakers who will never under any administration study the ways of the Ant or Honey Bee.

February. 1877.

*   *   *   *   *

It is over sixteen long years since I wrote Don's history for him, but Don shall not lose anything by that. Instead, I am now able to make Don a present of a chapter out of my own biography. Much good may it do him. It is good to be afflicted, therefore, I have no scruple about making Don a present of it. The sixteen years it represents, laid a heavy hand on myself. But they taught me to "paddle my own canoe." Moreover, my palms always itch intolerably to paddle the Frittaker canoes as well. I suppose this to be an idiosyncrasy of my character. The Frittakers hold it sheer inborn cussedness, closely akin to total depravity, if not the simon-pure article. However this may be, the Jay Cooke business, that under a Republican administration floored Don Frittaker, and sent him forth with a bran-new face, to live by beggary, robbery and outrage, set myself down in the valley of humiliation, and its sack cloth and ashes financially.

Out of a large amount of property, only one small house and lot on which was a mortgage of one thousand five hundred dollars, and one hundred and sixty dollars cash was left. With which one hundred and sixty dollars in the basement of our mortgaged house, in the spring of 1878, I embarked in grocery store keeping. One hundred and sixty dollars won't buy much of anything. Interest, one hundred and twenty dollars per year ; taxes, eighty-one dollars. A childlike and bland young man, who was no Chinee, called the first month and looked the situation over. It was all on four short shelves and a shorter counter. He entered me in the fourteenth business class, eight dollars per year. And I was now all ready to tramp myself through the darkest period of the business depression that followed the great panic of '73. The prospect was so black, that I fancied I saw in its midnight gloom. Nebulæ and Constellations no astronomer ever heard tell of. What else I might have discovered, if there had been time for star-gazing, heaven knows, there was no time. I had already tramped in the domestic tread mill over forty years, and through all those years, it had been more or less hard, dirty work, nearly every day. Tramp, tramp ! But it wasn't altogether a circumstance to the tramping that now set in. It began in the morning at 4, or half after 4 o'clock, and lasted until 10,

11, or 12 at night, as circumstances dictated. Those circumstances consisted, in part, of various trampings to a leading auction house, where in those days, ten dollars' worth of a bankrupt stock could be bought for a dollar. Standing or tramping there from 10 o'clock in the morning, until 4 in the afternoon, without a drop of water to drink, or a crumb to eat, and tramp home, often carrying packages weighing 20 or 25 pounds, hiring some kind of a vehicle if the amount exceeded this, get home and face my waiting impatient customers, and supply their wants. As a rule, it was 12 at night when those speculative picnics were over. And hard life as that was for a woman, I knew others had harder lives. I still know such, and like myself, they prefer such a hard life to either tramping, or in any other way robbing and cheating other people for a living. By such toilsome method, I increased largely my paltry stock, and diligence brought its usual reward. There is a great number of good, honest people still left in the world. My good neighbors sympathized with my endeavors to earn my living and pay my debts. My trade grew apace. I was able to meet all obligations as they fell due. The Frittakers, both branches, came and went. But I knew them of old, and they didn't, with their store books, gather in much of my worldly goods.

Well, I tramped and turned and went on ; and only think of it, every Frittaker hadn't one glass of beer, nor one drop of whiskey. No, it's not a mistake. There is not a more reliable historical fact, or more trustworthy asseveration in all this history. Ah ! what do I hear, Don's history smells like whiskey all through ? Come, come, right here I must state that there is criticism that has reason in it, that is fair, that is just. But there is also criticism that is a provocation, an aggravation, and beyond the bounds of human endurance. Let all such critics beware. Keep their hands off ; their tongues off ; their pens off ; criticism that will cheapen Don and cheapen Don's history, I'll neither endure nor tolerate.) And it is also true that the money beer and whiskey would have cost helped to pay off the mortgage and every cent of interest and taxes. I floored them all, Don, they didn't floor me. And did it simply with sobriety, industry and economy. And when, at the end of eight weary years, it was all over, and I balanced my books and declared a dividend, I found that my own wages had been just seventy-eight cents per day, my boarding and about twenty-five dollars' worth of clothing included. All the rest had gone into the mortgage, interest, taxes and the Frittaker baskets. I could have earned one dollar and twenty-five cents and my boarding at a wash tub, with nine hours labor and without a tithe of the care, perplexity and anxiety that almost maddened me. And you and the other mechanics who tramped into the headquarters of the mackerel bones, and who I have no doubt have been tramping ever since, could have earned at least two dollars and fifty cents per day working nine hours daily, and could have been well-to do, respectable citizens by this time, if it hadn't been for beer and whiskey, gambling, and other bad habits about which you know the most and tell the least.

And when yourself and the other Frittakers, your gospel in hand, come
around to divide up that 78 cents per day with me, I do hereby in black
and white solemnly depose, assoverate and promise you a Donnybrook Fair
that will far away eclipse that last picnic you enjoyed in the early days of
the Jay Cooke business, one that none of the real original Donnybrooks in
ould Ireland ever excelled.   And moreover, as it will be the first one I ever
gave you and the last one you will desire to get at my hands, I will myself
see to it that the new body the old Dutch surgeon at the West Penn will
devise and invent for you, does in every particular match your new face
exactly, so that thereafter you may be all of one piece, so to speak, Don,
and not a cheap patching up of some kind simply to get you off his hands.
And here I must state for your further benefit that the obstacles and difficulties I floored arose under a Republican administration, and under a Republican administration I floored them, and for 78 cents per day, which lat-
ter fact does not cheapen me in the least in my own estimation; nor does
the fact that I wheeled many a sack of flour up the street or down the street
to my customers do so; nor the fact that I wore brogans almost like the pair
the Irishman showed you, only there were no hob nails in mine; nor does
the sun bonnet, tow cloth apron and dress patched three ply under the el-
bows humiliate me.   When I think of them I shall remember them all, my
life with pride.   But what my humiliation would be to-day if I, in a country
like ours teeming with golden opportunities and cheap abundance, had squan-
dered in drunken debauchery all my earnings and then tramped up and down
begging and stealing the hard earnings of other people, I cannot conceive, let
alone describe, Don Frittaker.   But I can and do assure you that if I could
write a history like Henry Thomas Buckle's, or poetry like John Milton's, I
would not be half so proud of either as I am of my victory over the great
financial disaster of my life, a victory gained without assistance from any
quarter.

Because of the Jay Cooke business I never yet could publish Don's history for him.   It's too bad, but its better late than never.   I assure Don
and everybody else that my desire to publish it has never diminished in the
least.   And I do it now with all my heart.   And if when Don reads it, he
desires to have it further amplified, I'll do that, too, for Don.   I'll not, if I
can help it, have Don's history come to any kind of lame conclusion.   On
the contrary I'm going to do Don proud.   I have learned that there is in
the Woman's Department of the great Columbian Fair a library, and in it
there is a niche for the literary escapades of self-educated women; and as all
the literary education I have I acquired by diligent if rather desultory study
at home, in the occasional pauses in the toils, cares and trampings of my lot,
I claim to be a self-educated woman and one that can't be beaten in the mat- .
ter of literary escapades.   So I have applied for space in the aforesaid niche
for this volume.   And if any critic prowling around and through that niche
should upon examination of it feel in duty bound to tear me all to pieces,
and then and there annihilate myself and Don's history, I beg him or her to

consider well the fact that I have not written two volumes of introduction to Don's history. Have in fact for peace sake written no introduction whatever to Don's history. And moreover, with the most praiseworthy forebearance, have printed only a score or so of poems instead of dumping a Websters unabridged dictionary of them out of the press upon afflicted humanity. Let everybody, especially the critical ones, consider well what they have escaped, and forgive me the wrong I have done in consideration of the wrong I didn't do.

.

Mr. Gander.

Mr. Gander wanted to borrow one hundred dollars from me this morning. I excused myself by assuring Mr. Gander that I couldn't lend him one hundred cents, let alone one hundred dollars, which may be true or it may not. If it is not, if my assurance to Mr. Gander was a lie, I feel no compunction. In previous business transactions between myself and Mr Gander, Mr. Gander told me a multitude of lies, and they were premeditated lies deliberately told, and for the dishonest purpose of taking advantage of me in the value of the goods he was selling me; in short, for the express purpose of cheating me. Yet I don't hold Mr. Gander responsible for the lies he told me and everybody who dealt with him. I hold the State and its legislation responsible for the lying of us both. Mr. Gander may have set out in an honest career with the best of honest intentions. I don't know anything about how Mr. Gander set out in his career. I never knew Mr. Gander at all until he came peddling round with his peddling wagon piled full of barrels and baskets that contained a varied assortment of farm and garden produce, but he didn't produce them himself. Heaven forefend that the farming and gardening population should betake themselves to the marketing practices and principles of Mr. Gander. No, Mr. Gander bought his stock always, if possible, he assured me, from the producer. And that I believed very well, for the granger is often a greenhorn and no match for Mr. Gander, and were he a credulous granger, Mr. Gander would assuredly be a gainer and the granger a loser in whatever transactions they had with each other. But I inferred Mr. Gander couldn't always buy from the producer, for a great deal of Mr. Gander's stock had a travelled look. The wilted, yellow radish leaves told of the earlier spring of "Ole Virginny Shore," or "Maryland, My Maryland"; so did his wilted beans and peas. The wilting he deplored as an effect of the sun when I suggested the ravages of time. He demonstrated at once, in the most lucid as well as voluble manner, that time didn't affect them that way, and I, having provoked the controversy and seeing no sign that he would weary of it soon, cut it short by bargaining for a barrel of potatoes. And when we settled on the price, he proposed to donate the barrel, but nothing would serve my turn but have them measured in my own measure, which he did with alacrity, apparently cheerful, whether it was honestly so I no more know than I know about his early intentions. The intention and purpose of his lying I believe to be, in a great measure, the consequence of that legislation that places a high premium on dishonesty and lying by securing the rogue who practices both in peaceful possession of the goods or money he secures thereby. If Mr. Gander set out an honest man, he soon found himself being robbed on every hand by dishonest men. And he soon found there was no legal or other redress. Self-preservation is the predominant human instinct, so Mr. Gander, as was natural in a weak moral nature, succumbed to the temptation to plunder others as he had himself been plundered, seeing he could do it with impunity. And so I hold the State legislation responsible for Mr. Gander's lying and cheating; and also responsible that I myself deliberately and willfully, and without the least compunction, lied to Mr. Gander. It was simply a measure of self-protection against the law that urged Mr. Gander to rob me, and would have aided and abetted Mr. Gander in robbing me had I permitted him to rob me. And I assure everybody that I did in no wise deceive Mr. Gander, for Mr. Gander didn't believe a word of my statement. Mr. Gander knew I could have lent him a hundred dollars if I had been willing to lend it Mr. Gander's countenance gave no intimation of Mr. Gander's incredulity, nor did Mr. Gander's demeanor. Mr. Gander smiled suavely, talked genially of the business outlook and the crop prospect, told a good anecdote, laughed merrily, bowed politely and departed. Would it have been better for me to tell Mr. Gander the truth, that I could lend him the money but I wouldn't? That I knew him too well to lend him any money, even on the best security. That I knew that as soon as the time stipulated for paying me my money came around, and I, perhaps, having pressing need of my money, and Mr. Gander also, still having pressing need of it, or having it so employed that it paid him more than the interest he paid me, the astute Mr. Gander would not give either credence or consideration to my pressing demand for my money. Nay, if he knew well that I was subjected to serious loss by his withholding my money, that would neither touch the feelings or conscience of Mr. Gander. The recollection of the fact that I loaned him the money to save him from loss in a great strait would arouse no compunction in Mr. Gander. But Mr. Gander would prevaricate, would procrastinate. Mr. Gander would do this, not only because he was making money by keeping me out of my money, but because also my asking to have my money back as soon as due nettled Mr. Gander. "You're in a devil of a hurry," thought Mr. Gander. Then as my appeal brought no response, and I repeated it somewhat testily, Mr. Gander would grow bitterly indignant, would say to himself, "Why, now, for your impudence, I'll pay you so soon as I can't help it." And when we met would deplore the tightness of the money market and the meanness and dishonesty of those whom he trusted, and who didn't pay him, and maybe wouldn't pay him at all, and the gist of it all would be that as soon as those who wouldn't pay at all paid up, Mr. Gander would pay me. Now if I, poor wretch, caught in a trap like this and boiling over with indignation, would enter legal proceedings, what would I gain. Nobody outside the legal profession is better versed in legal tactics or better able to avail himself of the intricacies of the law than Mr. Gander. Over and over Mr. Gander has been sued, and every

time it did Mr. Gander good every time it did the prosecutor harm.   If
we could suppose that there are men in business who never swear at all, and
the men who prosecuted Mr. Gander never swore at all, it availed nothing.
They fell to swearing right away after they prosecuted Mr. Gander.   Mr.
Gander proved so adroit on the day fixed for trial, Mr. Gander's most important witness failed to show up, so did Mr. Gander, because Mr. Gander
went as usual after his business and let the prosecutor go to court and lose
his time, and let his attorney (he hired him by the year) stave off proceedings
until to-morrow or some other day, when the prosecutor again went to court
and lost his time and Mr. Gander didn't; and on this occasion, if Mr. Gander's important witness produced himself, some other body or something
else caused another stave off until some other day.   All the time Mr. Gander goes after his business, lying as usual, and his prosecutor goes around
swearing, whether usual or unusual.   And at the end of two or three
months of this, after having nearly swamped his soul in blasphemy, he
gladly pays the costs to be quit of the whole business.   Thinks
no more of the loss of his money or goods, whichever led him to prosecute
Mr. Gander, nor of the heavy cost and loss of time; thinks of nothing but
the joy of being quit of Mr. Gander.   Knowing all this, am I going first to
lend my money to Mr. Gander, and last to prosecute Mr. Gander?   I hold
it far wiser, far better, far safer to lie to Mr. Gander.   I only hoist Mr.
Gander with his own petard, I only foil him with his own weapons. And he
knows it all the while, and I all the while know that Mr. Gander's business
principles contain no fine sentiments of honor and sacred obligation.   Hedging,
as he would call it, to avoid paying money it is profitable to use.   Escaping
out of business difficulties and dangers by dragging the unwary in, are not
moral derelictions in Mr. Gander's estimation, but master strokes of business
finesse, something to be proud of. Dishonor! Dishonesty! Oh, get out, you
miserable saphead, thinks Mr. Gander; do you think I'd go to the trouble
of borrowing your paltry hundred dollars unless I could make it pay, and
pay well ?   If I could keep the whole amount I would be a fool not to keep
it.   Such are Mr. Gander's business principles and tactics.   I discovered
them in course of business transactions with Mr. Gander.   In his manner
and conversation Mr. Gander is very plausible ; very suave and genial in
business.   This is all with a view to concealing his principles and tactics.
Nevertheless, it led me at the outset to suspect the nature of his tactics.
As a measure of self-protection, I proceeded at once to buy on credit from
Mr. Gander, and then proceeded to lament to Mr. Gander that our nefarious
exemption laws released rogues from all liability in the matter of paying
their debts.   Is it not too bad, Mr. Gander, said I, by way of peroration,
that I need never pay you a cent for all this stock of vegetables and fruit
unless I think fit ? Mr. Gander never looked as bland as he did this morning,
but he saw, I knew myself master of the situation.   Mentally he swore con-
siderably, no doubt, for Mr. Gander is neither meek nor patient.   And his
mental objurgations were none the less deep that I confidentially informed

him that one of my business tactics was to weigh and measure and count everything I purchased ; no hap-hazard methods for me ; if I bought a pound I didn't want fifteen ounces ; if I got only fifteen I would pay for fifteen only.   Mr. Gander smiled genially as ever, assured me that was his invariable practice, bowed himself out, and sent me next day the barrel of potatoes.   Three bushels I had ordered, said the bill, and I had his boy empty and measure them—two bushels and three pecks of potatoes, and one peck of dirt which I put carefully away for Mr. Gander. . Perfectly right, that's that devilish boy's doings : shovels up dirt and everything—I wonder there wasn't a bushel of it, said Mr. Gander.   But I charged Mr. Gander the price of potatoes for that dirt, whether right or wrong, and deducted it from his bill ; and Mr. Gander vowed he would break that boy's neck as soon as he got home.   Presently an agent for a trustworthy house came along and I forthwith paid Mr. Gander every cent I owed Mr. Gander, and Mr. Gander don't owe me one, nor is Mr. Gander going to owe me one, for it is my fixed determination that this exemption from all indebtedness between myself and Mr. Gander must and will last forever and a day.   Had I candidly stated all this to Mr. Gander, Mr. Gander would have phoophooed and offered to credit me any amount ; to loan me five hundred dollars if I wanted it ; would have assured me that he knew me to be honesty and veracity itself.   Other people's slanders had prejudiced me against him ; that he had never cheated anybody in the world, never thought of doing so. Honest, honest Iago !   Yet knowing Mr. Gander's business principles, and knowing Mr. Gander's business practices, and knowing that the laws of my State, Pennsylvania, incites and urges Mr. Gander to be a rogue and a cheat, and to cheat me if he can ; and causes Mr. Gander to lose money by being honest, and rewards him liberally for being a rascal, in that he can legally hold fast to all the plunder he obtains by lying and cheating ; and, moreover, plants a banner of stripes and stars over my head and assures me that I am brave and free, yet delivers me a slave to Mr. Gander the minute I loan him one hundred dollars, and obliges me to take refuge in the slave's subterfuge of lying, makes me a lying poltroon to, if possible, save my money.   I, knowing all this, know enough to keep my money out of the clutches of Mr. Gander.

The Next Columbian Fair.

≈≈≈≈≈≈

"What will it be?" people ask. And I, who am one of those who know everything and am always willing to tell everybody, come promptly to the front, but not feeling half so cheerful as I would like to feel to answer the question. It will never be at all. When the time to hold it comes around, this land of ours will be the habitat of the owls and the bats and a prowling multitude of naked savages to whom the extinct red men were not a circumstance in the matter of savage, murderous cussedness and unmitigated worthlessness. Is it any wonder I don't feel cheerful? "'Tis the sunset of life gives me mystical lore." "And the coming events that cast their shadows before" are as follows: Our present legislation is simply the drooling of idiots, and an embodiment of the want of all good principle in the traitorous knaves we know as political demagogues. They embody it for a class whose vote they covet, as the said vote provides fat sinecures, with fatter salaries, for the aforesaid demagogues. This legislation is a standing conflict with the Constitution of the United States, and has no relation to justice, and outrages common sense; is simply a premium upon meanness, laziness, dirtiness, wastefulness, lying, false pretense, fraud, extravagance, intemperance, gambling, debauchery, and extinguishes honor, honesty, sturdy independence, self-respect, self restraint; in short, everything that makes the sum and substance of an honorable, upright man or woman, and incites, even urges such to become sniffling, snuffling, sneaking beggars and paupers; and those with an inborn tendency that way, to red-handed, murderous crime, holds out every inducement for them to keep the straight road to the palatial poor-houses and penitentiaries it provides for them. No nation whose legislation embodies such principles, no people that accepts and puts them into practice, and lives in the practice of them, can long exist as a people and a nation. The outcome must, of necessity, be anarchy, common, utter, irretrievable ruin. Especially must this ensue where the majority is determined to enslave the minority ; is bent upon depriving its members of every right, public and private, in their business and property, and obliges them to hold both, solely for the interest and profit of the ruling majority which assumes all oversight and control, dictates the methods pursued, the hours, the amount of proceeds, the division of proceeds throughout all its ramifications, own and control in everything, except in the first place buying it and furnishing the capital to support it. For that, and that only, would they tolerate the minority. While their demagogue tools grind out the legislation that vests entire control and ownership of all goods and tenement property in their legal enactments, that, of course, represent the State itself. What else does it mean for these laws to make a present of 45 days' free occupancy of a dwelling to the contemptible rogue who has, by lying promises to pay his rent, already occupied it 4, 5 or 6 months free of all costs? What does this mean, if it don't mean that the State owns the property, not the man who, with his family, toiled and economized for years to earn the money to pay for it? What does it mean, if it don't mean that the owner is the slave of the rogue who is occupying his house in whole or in part, and robbing him by doing so? If the State does not own the goods the merchant holds in possession, what does it mean that any lying cheat that, by plausible representation of ability to pay, obtains possession of more or less of them is, by the State, protected fully in refusing to pay for them, and in never paying for them? What right has the State to do this with those goods if they are the citizen's own private property, and not the State's? Since the evil day when a wily political demagogue, with a keen eye to the vote of the workingmen, introduced and secured the passage of an act exempting three hundred dollars' worth of goods from seizure for debt; since that legislature placed that high premium upon dishonesty, honor and honesty have, in this good Commonwealth of Pennsylvania, gone to the dogs. All merchants, and especially retail dealers, can testify that through this legal act the merchant trade loses annually millions of dollars. If any one doubt this, let him interview all tradesmen, especially retail tradesmen and tenement property owners, landlords, grocers, butchers, bakers, dairymen, shoemakers, tailors, everybody, druggists, doctors, undertakers; rogues don't pay for even their shrouds and coffins when they can make other people do it. Interview them all, and you will learn appalling facts. As a means of degrading and demoralizing the people, this law is unexcelled even by beer and whiskey, and under its ruling beer and whiskey have grown rampant. For now, those addicted to their intemperate use can and do spend nearly all they earn upon them, and support their families by robbing their landlords and retail dealers, anybody and everybody who is so unfortunate as to credit them. For these last there is no redress whatever; in fact, our demagogue legislation evidently relegates them to the ranks of the malefactors who, having no rights, cannot be wronged; holds them as custodians only of whatever may be in their possession, and he, who can by any manner of lying or false pretense obtain possession of it, is rightfully the legal owner. Such is the nature and such is the effect of this villainous law that has been trumpeted through the land as a benefaction to the working people. Since the first hour of its active existence it has proven unmitigated diabolism; has done more to corrupt, degrade and debauch them than all other causes put together. None but persons who, like myself, were engaged in retail business, both before and since its passage, can have any just conception of the deplorable change it has wrought. Under its fostering influence gambling and profligacy is becoming universal among young men. They move from boarding house to boarding house, and obtain their food and lodging for almost nothing, and in a similar manner they rob one dealer and another of the clothing they wear, while squandering their earnings at the bar and the gaming table and even worse resorts. Land monopolies, railroad monopolies, every great combination of capital, is certainly dangerous to the best interest of all classes, but they never, never, can rob the people, like the legislation that robs them, of honor and honesty, by releasing them from the sacred obligations of both, and offering them a reward of three hundred dollars for renouncing both and practicing open, undisguised robbery. What the working man and the people at large need worst at present is the immediate repeal of every legal enactment that is a premium upon dishonesty. Oblige him and everybody to pay for everything they purchase. This, as a rule, will leave far less money for drinking, gambling and debauchery to those who spend their money on these degrading vices. Oblige them to live upon their own earnings, and this, of necessity, will turn their attention to the practice of economy. If our working people were the prudent, thrifty, virtuous people they ought to be, dwelling in homes that are their own property and free of debt, our working people could dictate their own terms to capital. But a man who has no home and who, when emergencies arise, never has a dollar saved to meet them with, is poorly equipped for a tournament with capital. And when a thousand of such men are precipitated into the ring their numbers are not strength but multiplied weakness that means defeat and calamitous loss, will leave them weaker and poorer, and capital stronger and richer when the tilt is over. Prudence and economy are the best and only safeguards of the working people against the encroachments of capital, and honesty is for all classes the true source of prosperity. I do not mean honesty restricted by law to the working class, while merchants and manufacturers go into bankruptcy and, protected by our diabolical legislation, repudiate every debt and sacred obligation that honor binds a man to pay if it take his last cent and cent's worth, and then with their families continue to live in unabated extravagance and luxury with the proceeds of the robbery. While nearly every square of every city in the land contains a specimen of such unabashed villainy, what better can we expect than what we have of our working people? In all ages and among all people the higher class has been the model copied by the lower class. Equality before the law is one of the fundamental principles of our law, and demands that law—like justice—be even handed. When misfortunes overwhelm a workingman he must, empty handed, when the storm is over, begin life anew. Let the merchant and manufacturer do the same. Could we trace through the intricate windings of trade and manufacture, business depressions and panics to their inceptive causes, we would reach the momentous fact that extravagance, waste and intemperance are the chief causes of dishonesty, and dishonesty's unpaid bills the chief causes of depressions and panics. And, moreover, if merchants and manufacturers were paid the vast sums they lose through the pernicious credit system they would doubtless be both more able and more willing to pay high wages.   But high wages alone will never improve the condition of the working people, nor ever in the world enable them to cope successfully with capital.   Only when they have higher aspirations than gluttonous eating and intemperate drinking, when they value honor and honesty as they do their lives, scorn dishonesty and beggary, take pride in prudence and economy and the ownership of their own homes and in their own intelligence and refinement, will the working people be the ruling power, the country permanently prosperous, and the next Great Columbian Fair a possibility.